TABLE OF CONTENTS

SECTION 1

A LOOK AT THE STORM TIDES IN TWELVE TROPICAL CYCLONES INCLUDING FOUR INTENSE NEW ENGLAND HURRICANES

BRIAN JARVINEN (RETIRED)

NOAA/TROPICAL PREDICTION CENTER/NATIONAL HURRICANE CENTER

OCTOBER 1, 2006

INTRODUCTION

The United States Atlantic and Gulf of Mexico coastlines have repeatedly been modified and reshaped by hurricane storm tides over the years. Since the arrival of immigrants from Europe, the coastline has steadily been developed with the addition of many homes and other buildings and an ever increasing coastal population. The consequences of this increase are visible, with each passing year, as hurricanes make landfall at different locations. However, for a specific location along the coast the frequency of an intense hurricane impact is low. Decades may pass between intense storms and in some locations such as New England; there may be hundreds of years between storms. Having an accurate historical data base on the most intense hurricanes is one of the main goals of hurricane research. One of the problems until the advent of reconnaissance flights into hurricanes in the 1940's was determining an intensity at landfall. Early sixteen and seventeen hundred eye-witness accounts of destruction from wind forces tell us little about the intensity. When wind and pressure measuring sensors began appearing in the nineteenth and twentieth centuries they rarely measured near the core of a hurricane where the maximum winds occur. Even when they were in the right place to measure the strongest winds, the device or its support mechanism failed. This problem still plagues us today. Some historical hurricanes had sea-level pressure readings taken as the center passed over and are excellent measures of the intensity. However, almost all of the historical accounts make reference to elevated water levels. Since these water levels are generated by the wind and pressure forces in the hurricane it is yet another measure of intensity. So if one can use a combined storm surge and astronomical tide model and reproduce the observed high water levels then one can deduce the intensity; both sea-level pressure in the eye as well as the maximum wind speed. This will be done for several of the early hurricanes, specifically the Great Colonial hurricane of 1635 and the Great September Gale of 1815. Two other intense hurricanes that impacted New England will also be analyzed: the 1938 hurricane and hurricane Carol in 1954. Seven additional hurricanes and one tropical storm will also be included and each will have its own section in this report.

The purpose of this report is to investigate the storm tides reported in each hurricane as well as the intensity at landfall. The hope is that this information will aid emergency management agencies at the federal, state and local level along with individuals residing along the coast to make proper life and property saving decisions when similar hurricanes threaten the region in the future.

PROCEDURE

Each hurricane will have a summary of available meteorological and hydrologic data. A discussion of the meteorological data and its use in determining the track, intensity and size (i.e. radius of maximum winds) will follow. Next, a numerical storm surge model will be used to simulate each hurricane's maximum storm surge for the region of interest. In addition, a tide prediction program will also be used to determine the stage of the astronomical tide during the storm surge event so that an accurate comparison can be made to high water marks, which are a combination of both phenomena. Finally, a table showing a comparison of the maximum storm surge and intensity of the hurricanes will be made. First, a brief description and discussion of the dominant water elevating forces present in a hurricane will be made as well as the high water marks that they produce. Also, a description of the numerical storm surge model will be made.

STORM SURGE

Storm surge is the abnormal rise of water caused by the wind and pressure forces in a hurricane. The dominant of these two forces is the wind. Some of the wind's energy is transferred to the water to form waves. The waves, in turn, transfer some of their energy downward to form currents. In the deep ocean these currents rotate about the hurricane with little effect on water elevation. However, as the hurricane tracks toward a coastline, it first encounters the continental shelf and the currents, especially on the right side of the hurricane, begin to be slowed and compressed resulting in a rise of water which is the storm surge. As the hurricane continues toward landfall at the coastline and moves inland, the process continues and the height of the storm surge increases. In addition, the funneling or squeezing effect of bays and estuaries enhances the storm surge and in many cases the maximum heights are found at the heads of these bays and estuaries. This will readily become apparent from the data and analyses of these hurricanes.

ASTRONOMICAL TIDE OR TIDE AND MEAN SEA LEVEL

The astronomical tide, or tide for short, is an oscillation in the ocean caused by the gravitational attraction of the moon and sun on the earth. For most of the east coast of the United States the tide is semi-diurnal. This means that generally there are two high tides and two low tides each day. People living on or near the coast are usually aware of how high and how low these tide levels reach. This was especially true in the early colonial period when almost all travel was done by ship, boat and canoe. The tides, with their associated tidal currents, helped or hindered travel. Somewhat more difficult to locate is the mid-point of the tide or mean tide. The mean tide location is closely related to mean sea level Mean sea level is often referenced as zero elevation for the land and for our purposes, the water surface also. So another way of looking at the tide is that it oscillates up and down relative to mean sea level. For example, if the tide rose from low tide to high tide and the vertical distance traveled was four feet, then we could also say that it rose from minus two feet below mean sea level to plus two feet above mean sea level.

In 1929, mean sea level was determined using tide gage records along the North American coastlines. This was called the North Atlantic Vertical Datum of 1929 or NGVD for short. All land elevations were referenced to this datum. In our example above the tide would have risen from minus two feet below NGVD to plus two feet above NGVD. We could have said that in 1929 but not today. Since 1929 sea level has been rising at about a foot per century. So the current location of mean sea level in 2006 is about 0.75 feet above NGVD. If a building's elevation was measured at ten feet above NGVD then today it would only be 9.25 feet above mean sea level. In 1988 a new datum was created to give an accurate vertical reference at any location. It is termed the North Atlantic Vertical Datum of 1988 or NAVD88. It is not a correction for rising mean sea level because at most locations there can be a significant difference between the two. But it is an accurate datum to measure the changes in mean sea level in the future.

STORM TIDE

The combination of hurricane generated storm surge and the tide is called the storm tide. Because of the nature and size of the forces generating these two phenomena, they act almost independent of one another. Thus, if a hurricane creates a storm surge of 10 feet at a location on the coast, the 10 feet will occur no matter what part of the oscillation the tide is in. In our tide example above, if the tide is high (plus 2 feet msl) and the storm surge maximum of 10 feet occurs, the storm tide will be 12 feet msl. On the other hand, if the tide is low (minus 2 feet msl) when the maximum occurs then the storm tide will be 8 feet msl. Since the tide could be anywhere in its oscillation the storm tide could range from 8 to 12 feet msl. Obviously, the worst case scenario is maximum storm surge occurring at high tide.

HIGH WATER ELEVATIONS

In many of the historical hurricanes, how the observer states the high water elevation is very important. For example, the observer may state that the water rose 10 feet above the normal tide level. In this case he is making reference to the storm surge. This would be good data with which to verify a storm surge model. However, since we do not know the tide level we can not determine the storm tide relative to msl. If we have a good storm surge model that can replicate the storm surge with time relative to msl (also called a storm surge hydrograph) and a tide prediction model that produces a tide hydrograph relative to msl, we can add the two together to come up with a storm tide hydrograph relative to msl. From this storm tide hydrograph, we can determine a maximum storm tide height at a particular location. The goal is to try and reference all of the high water marks in all the hurricanes relative to msl so a direct comparison can be made.

Another observation that is often found in historical descriptions is that the water rose 6 feet above the previous high water mark or 6 feet higher than any inhabitant can remember. Unfortunately, in almost all these cases we do not know what that previous high mark was. So this information has little quantitative value.

BREAKING WAVES

Riding on top of the storm surge are waves that have been generated by the winds. As these waves approach the coastline they begin to break and rush forward. Initially, when the storm tide is small these breaking waves have little impact on buildings and structures along the coastline. As the storm tide rises, the waves break closer to the shoreline. If the storm tide is high enough, the waves can break against and into the buildings and structures. This breaking wave energy is what destroys most of the buildings and structures along the coast. Thus, the storm tide is the mechanism to elevate the water level close to or into a structure so that the waves can damage or destroy them. Also important to note is that the wind continues to generate waves as long as it can "feel" the water so that the wave generation process continues even after inundation of dry land occurs. Most of the breaking wave energy is expended within several hundred feet of the original shoreline. This is referred to as the breaking wave zone. In this breaking wave zone, high water marks measured in buildings that survive may reflect a combination of storm tide height and breaking wave generated height. In shoreline studies, the breaking wave generated height is often referred to as an additional height due to the combination of wave set-up and wave run-up. If we wish a fair comparison of these hurricanes it will be important to remove the wave affected high water marks. (Note: Although it is useful to know these wave added heights for engineering taller and stronger structures in the breaking wave zone, it is not critical for hurricane evacuation studies because these zones are always evacuated.)

STORM SURGE MODEL

The storm surge model used is SLOSH which is an acronym for Sea, Lake and Overland Surges from Hurricanes, Jelesnianski, et al (1992). SLOSH is a numerical model and was developed by the National Oceanographic and Atmospheric Administration's (NOAA) National Weather Service (NWS) for operational forecasting. The model has also proven invaluable in determining the hurricane storm surge flood plain along the U.S. Atlantic and Gulf of Mexico coastlines prior to a hurricane landfall. This has led to comprehensive hurricane evacuation plans for both of these areas.

The SLOSH model, given hurricane input parameters, computes storm surge heights over a geographic area that is covered by a grid of computational points. This network, or model domain, is called a basin. At present, 35 basins cover the U.S. Atlantic and Gulf of Mexico coastal flood plains. Two of the basins that cover a large portion of New England have been designated the Narragansett/Buzzard Bay basin and the Boston Bay basin and are shown in Figures 1a and 1b. These two basins will be used in our look at four intense hurricanes that impacted this area. Other basins will be used for the remaining eight storms but will not be shown.

The SLOSH model requires hurricane input parameters at specified time intervals. These parameters include the latitude and longitude of the storm center, the atmosphere sea level pressure in the center and the radius of the maximum surface wind speed (RMW). These will be discussed for each storm.

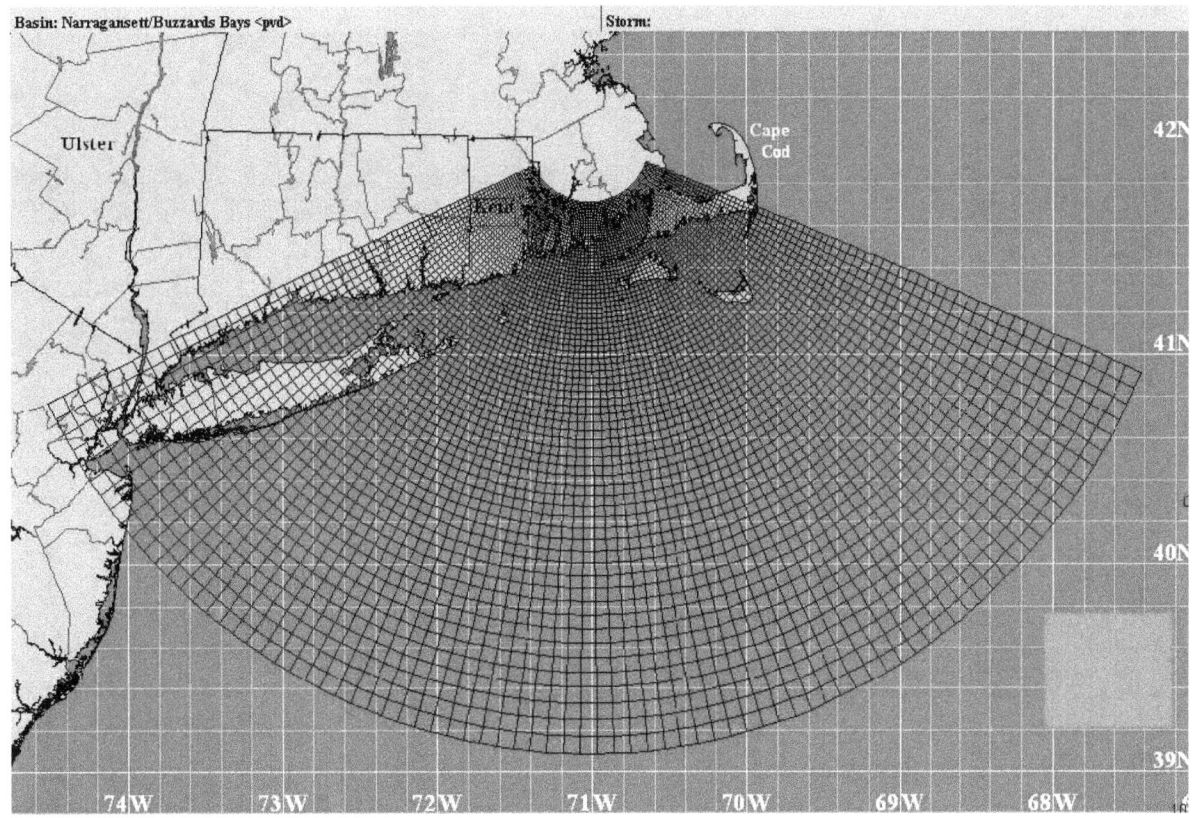

Figure 1a. Narragansett / Buzzard Bay Basin

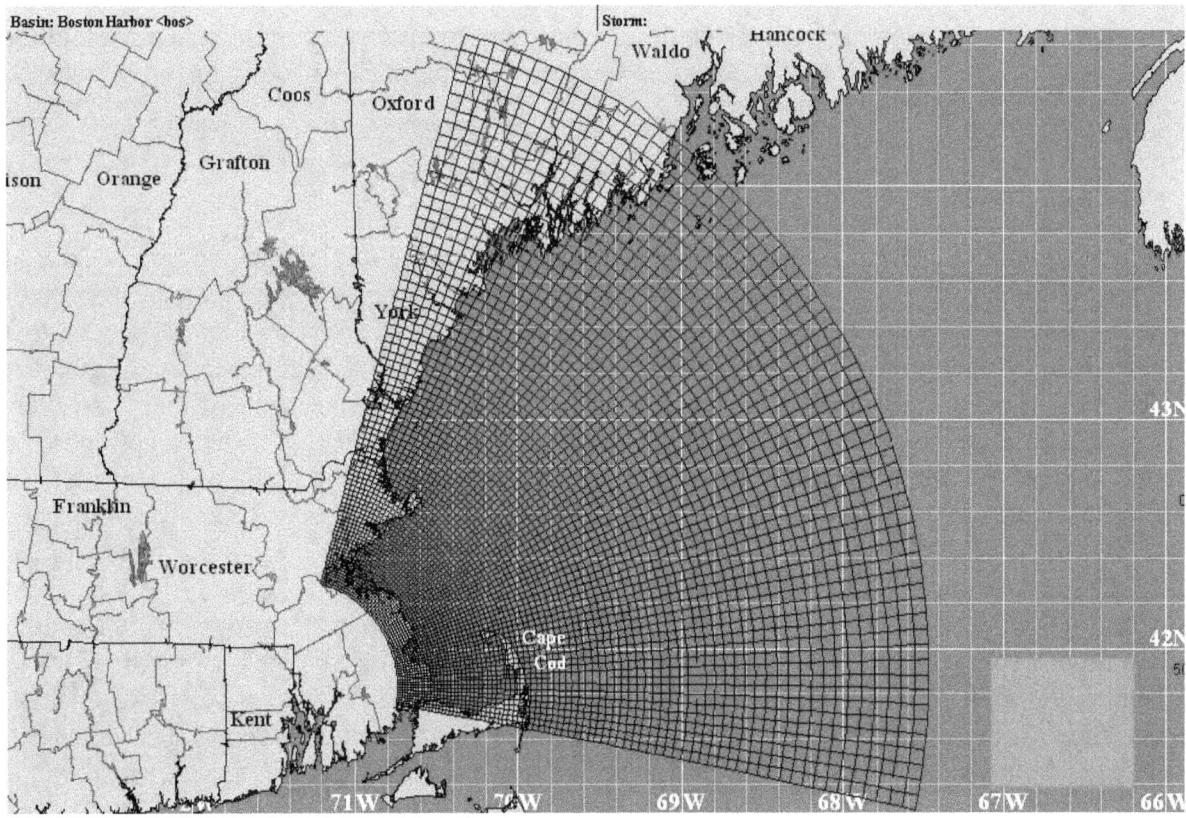

Figure 1b. Boston Bay Basin

SECTION 2

THE GREAT COLONIAL HURRICANE OF 1635

An excellent starting point is Ludlum's (1963) write-up of this hurricane. He first clears up the confusion of the dates used at the time and thus the day of landfall is the 26th of August, 1635. He cites two historians who gave accounts of this hurricane in published books. They are William Bradford (1647) of Plymouth Plantation and John Winthrop(1649) of Massachusetts Bay Colony. In today's world it would be like having an observer in Boston and Plymouth Massachusetts. The two accounts follow:

JOHN WINTHROP'S ACCOUNT

August 16 (Author's note: It should be the 26th of August). The wind having blown hard at S. and S.W. a week before, about midnight it came up at N.E. and blew with such violence, with abundance of rain, that it blew down many hundreds of trees, near the towns, overthrew some houses, and drove the ships from their anchors. The Great Hope, of Ipswich, being about four hundred tons, was driven aground at Mr. Hoffe's Point, and brought back again presently by a N. W. wind, and ran on shore at Charlestown. About eight of the clock the wind came about to N.W. very strong, and it being then about high water, by nine the tide had fallen three feet. Then it began to flow again about one hour, and rose about two or three feet, which was conceived to be, that the sea was grown so high abroad with a N.E. wind, that, meeting with the ebb, it forced it back again.

This tempest was not so far as Cape Sable, but to the south more violent, and made a double tide all that coast…The tide rose at Narragansett fourteen feet higher than ordinary, and drowned eight Indians flying from their wigwams.

WILLIAM BRADFORD'S ACCOUNT

This year, the 14th or 15th of August (being Saturday) (Author's note: It should be the 26th of August) was such a mighty storm of wind and rain as none living in these parts, either English or Indians, ever saw. Being like, for the time it continued, to those hurricanes and typhoons that writers make mention of in the Indies. It began in the morning a little before day, and grew not by degrees but came with violence in the beginning, to the great amazement of many. It blew down sundry houses and uncovered others. Divers vessels were lost at sea and many more in extreme danger. It caused the sea to swell to the southward of this place above 20 feet right up and down, and made many of the Indians to climb into trees for their safety. It took off the boarded roof of a house which belonged to this Plantation at Manomet, and floated it to another place, the posts still standing in the ground. And if it had continued long without the shifting of the wind, it is like it would have drowned some part of the country. It blew down many hundred thousands of trees, turning up the stronger by the roots and breaking the higher pine trees off in the middle. And the tall young oaks and walnut trees of good bigness were wound like a withe, very strange and fearful to behold. It began in the southeast and parted toward the south and east, and veered sundry ways, but the greatest force of it here was from the former quarters. It continued not (in the extremity) above five or six hours but the violence began to abate. The signs and marks of it will remain this hundred years where it was sorest. The moon suffered a great eclipse the second night after it.

I went back to the original published books to check for any additional information and found that an error exists in the Ludlum copy of Bradford's account which was corrected in this version. Bradford's states that "southward of this place" not "south wind of this place" as Ludlum states. This is significant in that it is referencing the head of Buzzards Bay and the incredible storm tide that occurred there. Also, the dates at the start of Bradford's account do not agree with the date for Winthrop's account. However, at the end of Bradford's account it states, "The moon suffered a great eclipse the second night after it." Astrological records show that a full eclipse occurred in New England on August 28, 1635. Thus, the 26 of August is the day of the hurricane relative to our modern calendar. Apparently, Bradford had lost a day somehow!

METEOROLOGICAL DATA

The accounts give very little information. The shifting of the winds suggests a track passing between Boston and Plymouth. The fact that, "About 8 of the clock the wind came about to the N.W. very strong," suggests that the center is in the Atlantic Ocean to the east of Boston at 8 am. This is where the 8 am position was placed.

Based upon these two accounts, Ludlam speculates that the track of the hurricane comes up from the south or southwest and moves, "across upper Narragansett Bay close to Providence, through the Massachusetts counties of Bristol and northern Plymouth, to enter Massachusetts Bay in Norfolk County on the South Shore somewhere near Cohasset." Cohasset is located just to the southeast of Boston. I agree with this hypothesis. In addition, there is reference to this hurricane affecting the Jamestown colony in Virginia, but not causing major damage except on the outer coast. Thus, the southern portion of the track would be shifted closer to the Virginia coast but remaining far enough off shore as to not affect the intensity of the hurricane.

The damage to structures and the loss of "hundred thousands of trees" is reminiscent of the descriptions in the 1938 hurricane so the intensity is comparable.

From Bradford's account, "It continued not (in the extremity) above five or six hours but the violence began to abate." This suggests a rapidly moving hurricane.

HYDROLOGIC DATA

From John Winthrop, "This tempest was not so far as Cape Sable, but to the south more violent, and made a double tide all that coast...The tide rose at Narragansett fourteen feet higher than ordinary, and drowned eight Indians flying from their wigwams." Double tide means a storm surge on top of the normal tide. The 14 feet is very likely all storm surge. The reference to Narragansett means Providence Plantation located near the current site of the city of Providence, Rhode Island.

From John Winthrop, "About eight of the clock the wind came about to N.W. very strong, and it being then about high water, by nine the tide had fallen three feet. Then it began to flow again about one hour, and rose about two or three feet, which was conceived to be, that the sea was grown so high abroad with a N.E. wind, that, meeting with the ebb, it forced it back again."

From William Bradford, "It caused the sea to swell to the southward of this place above 20 feet right up and down, and made many of the Indians to climb into trees for their safety." "Above 20 feet right up and down" is very impressive and southward of this place is somewhere at the head of Buzzards Bay.

SLOSH MODEL SIMULATION

In this hurricane there is not a specified set of input data for the SLOSH model. Therefore, we had to make our own. Initially, a hypothetical track, intensity and size were created. The track direction was similar to Ludlam's suggestion. The intensity was set to the 1938 hurricane's intensity and the hurricane was moved along the track at about 30 mph. The radius of maximum wind (RMW) was set at 30 st. mi. A series of SLOSH model runs were made, adjusting the various parameters until the two storm surge values of 14 feet and above 20 feet were matched. The final track is shown in Figure 2.1.

After passing by the Virginia coast this large category 4 hurricane continued to accelerate toward the northeast. Since the hurricane occurred in late August the sea surface temperatures were likely 80 degrees Fahrenheit or warmer up to about the latitude of southern New Jersey similar to hurricane Bob on the 19th of August, 1991. Bob's central pressure did not begin to rise until it reached this latitude. A similar thing is done with this hurricane except that the hurricane is 930 mb when it starts to fill. It makes its first landfall on eastern Long island with a central pressure of 938 mb and second landfall in Connecticut, just west of the Connecticut/Rhode Island border. It has a central pressure of 939 mb and is moving about 40 mph with a RMW of 35 st. mi. Figure 2.2 shows the track across New England. The hourly values of the center location are labeled in local standard time. Also, plotted next to each position is the central pressure and the SLOSH model's calculated maximum one-minute wind over the water. Generally, this maximum will be located on the right side of the track at the radius of maximum wind over the water. The hurricane races across New England and exits near Cohasset, as mentioned by Ludlam. The track direction and speed and storm size is almost optimum for generating the highest storm surge in Buzzards Bay and a significant storm surge in Narragansett Bay. Figure 2.3 shows the maximum storm surge throughout the two basins generated by the SLOSH model regardless of the time of the occurrence of the maximum. This is termed the storm surge envelope of high water. The lines in figure 2.3 represent the height of the storm surge in feet above mean sea level. Generally, the envelope of high water is compared against high water marks to determine the effectiveness of the model. Of course, in this case the two observed high water marks were used to determine the track and intensity and will be an almost perfect comparison. The location of the two observations and their value are also shown in the figure.

Examination of Figure 2.3 shows that the highest storm surge values occur at the heads of the bays. The storm surge elevations along the coastline in the Boston, Massachusetts and Cape Cod bays are on the order of 2 to 4 feet with maximums of 5.2 feet at Boston, 3.3 feet at Plymouth and 5.2 feet at Cape Cod. Some historical write-ups had put the 20 foot value in the Boston area. This puts to rest that misinformation. In fact, if that had really occurred we would probably not have had an account from either of the two historians. Closer examination of the results at the head of Buzzards Bay show that several other locations experienced values as high as 21 to 22 feet msl which may be why Bradford states the height as "above 20 feet". If this is the case, then this hurricane would have produced the highest storm surge on the eastern coast of the United States in recorded history. The current record is held by hurricane Hugo in 1989, with a landfall at Charleston, SC. It produced a storm tide of 20.1 feet msl near high tide or a storm surge of approximately 17.5 feet. The next step is to try and determine what the storm tide was. Unfortunately, at this writing the hindcast tide models available do not go back this far with reasonable certainty of getting the timing and amplitude of the tide correct. I had hoped that the observation made by Winthrop at Boston, "At 8 of the clock the wind came about to N.W. very strong, and it being then about high water, by nine the tide had fallen three feet....", was near high tide. But this may be a reference to the storm tide. As soon as the wind turned toward the northwest the water was being driven away from the coastline. As the hurricane moved rapidly toward the east-northeast the wind force on the water decreased and it began to return. Last but not least, the SLOSH generated storm surge hydrographs for Providence, the head of Buzzards Bay and Boston are shown as insets in Figure 2.3. What is striking about the hydrographs at Providence and the head of Buzzards Bay is the rapid rise and fall of the storm surge and Bradford's account is particularly graphic, "It caused the sea to swell to the southward of this place above 20 feet right up and down, and made many of the Indians to climb into trees for their safety."

SUMMARY FOR THE 1635 HURRICANE

The 1635 hurricane was a category 3.5 on the Saffir/Simpson scale. The central pressure was 938 mb near eastern Long Island and 939 mb to 941 mb as it passed through southern New England moving northeast at 40 mph. The RMW was 35 st. mi. Maximum observed storm surges were 14.0 feet at Providence, RI, above 20.0 feet at the head of Buzzards Bay, MA. SLOSH calculated storm surge values give 14.0 feet at Providence, above 20 feet at the head of Buzzards Bay and 2 to 4 feet along the eastern coast of Massachusetts. This was probably the most intense hurricane in New England history.

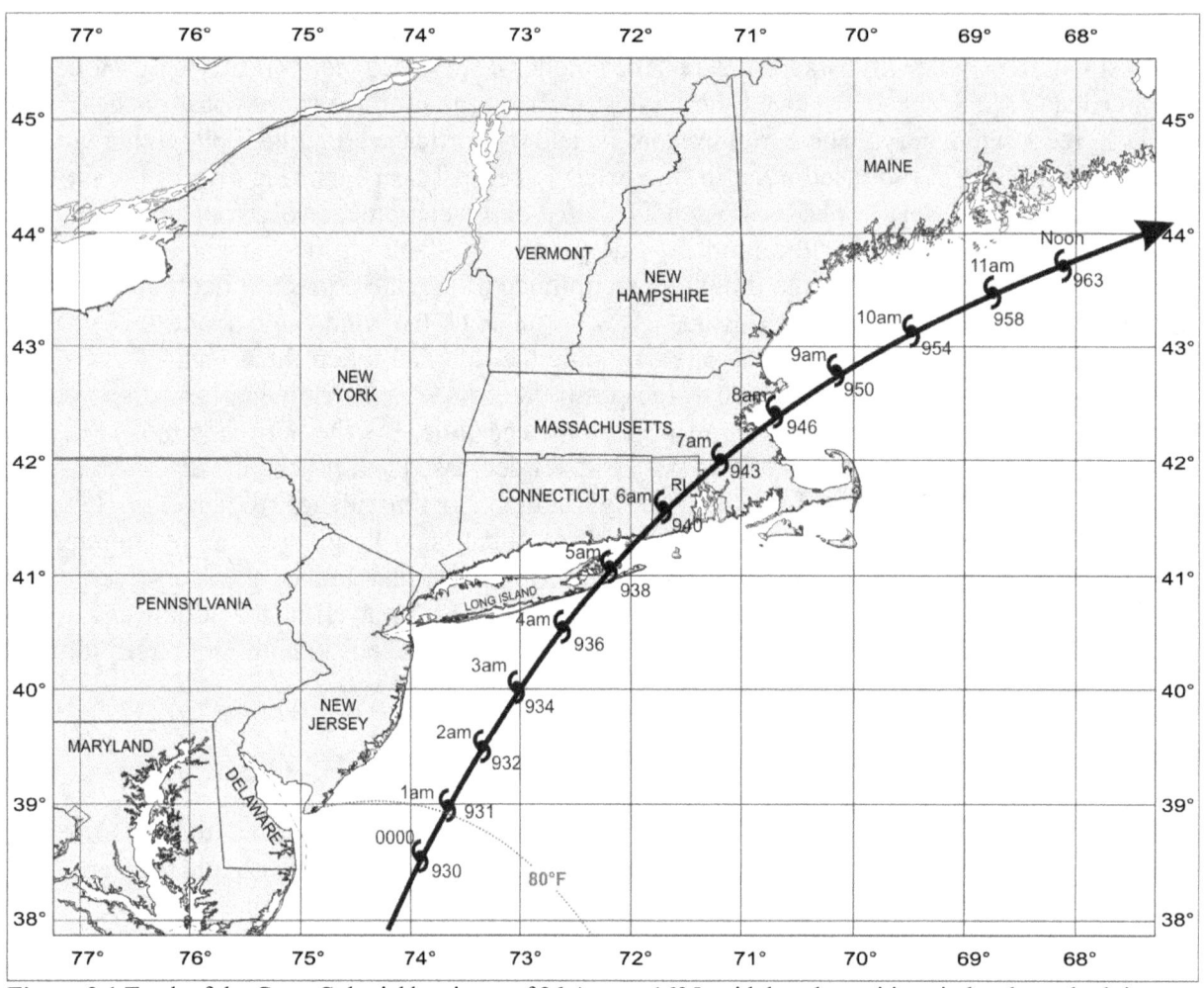

Figure 2.1 Track of the Great Colonial hurricane of 26 August 1635, with hourly positions in local standard time and central pressure in millibars. Possible 80°F SST isotherm also shown.

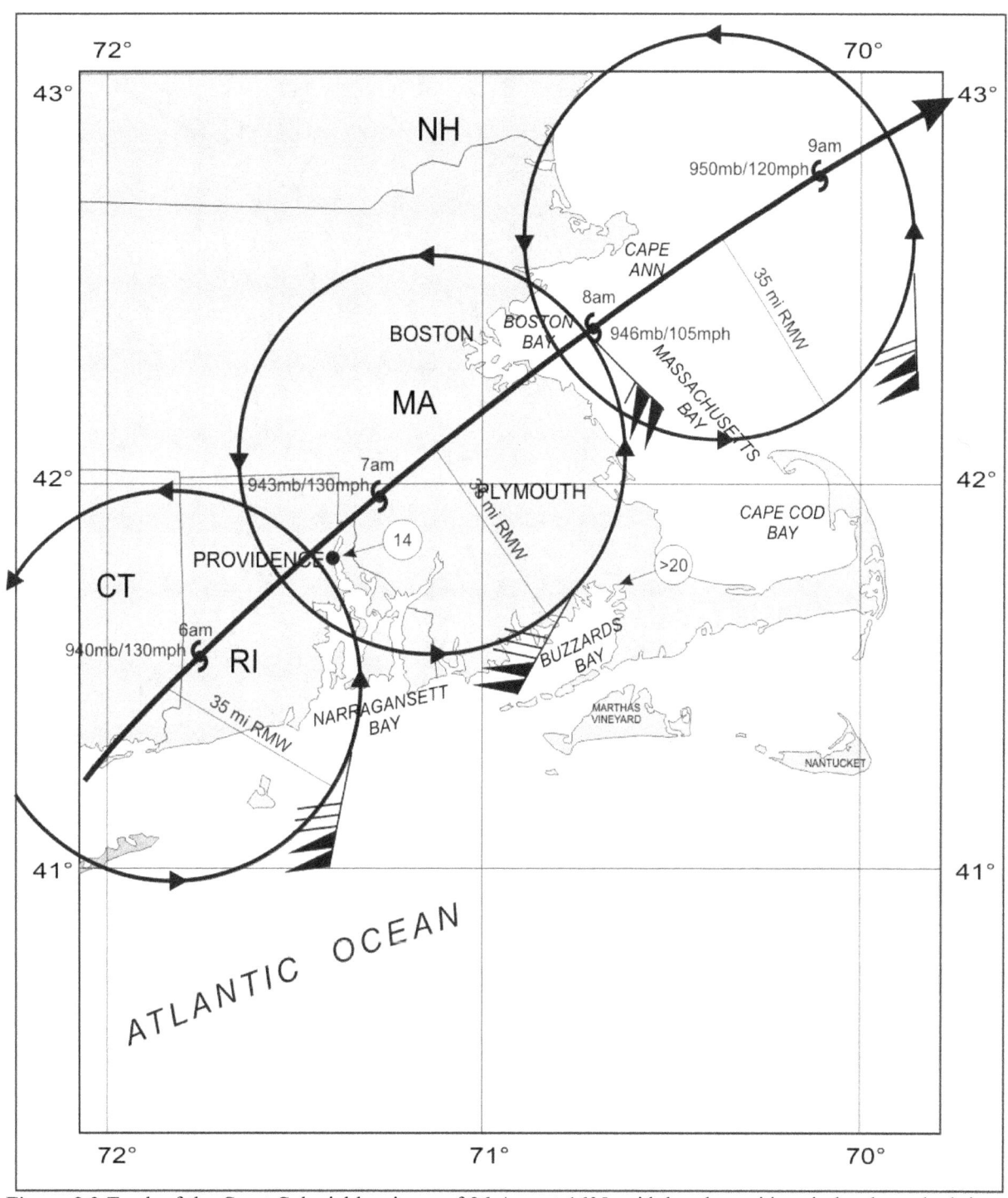

Figure 2.2 Track of the Great Colonial hurricane of 26 August 1635, with hourly positions in local standard time, pressure in millibars and SLOSH model maximum over water 1-minute wind speed in miles per hour. Circles represent location of maximum wind with radius given in statute miles. Wind vectors show where maximum wind is occurring at that time. Wind barbs in mph.

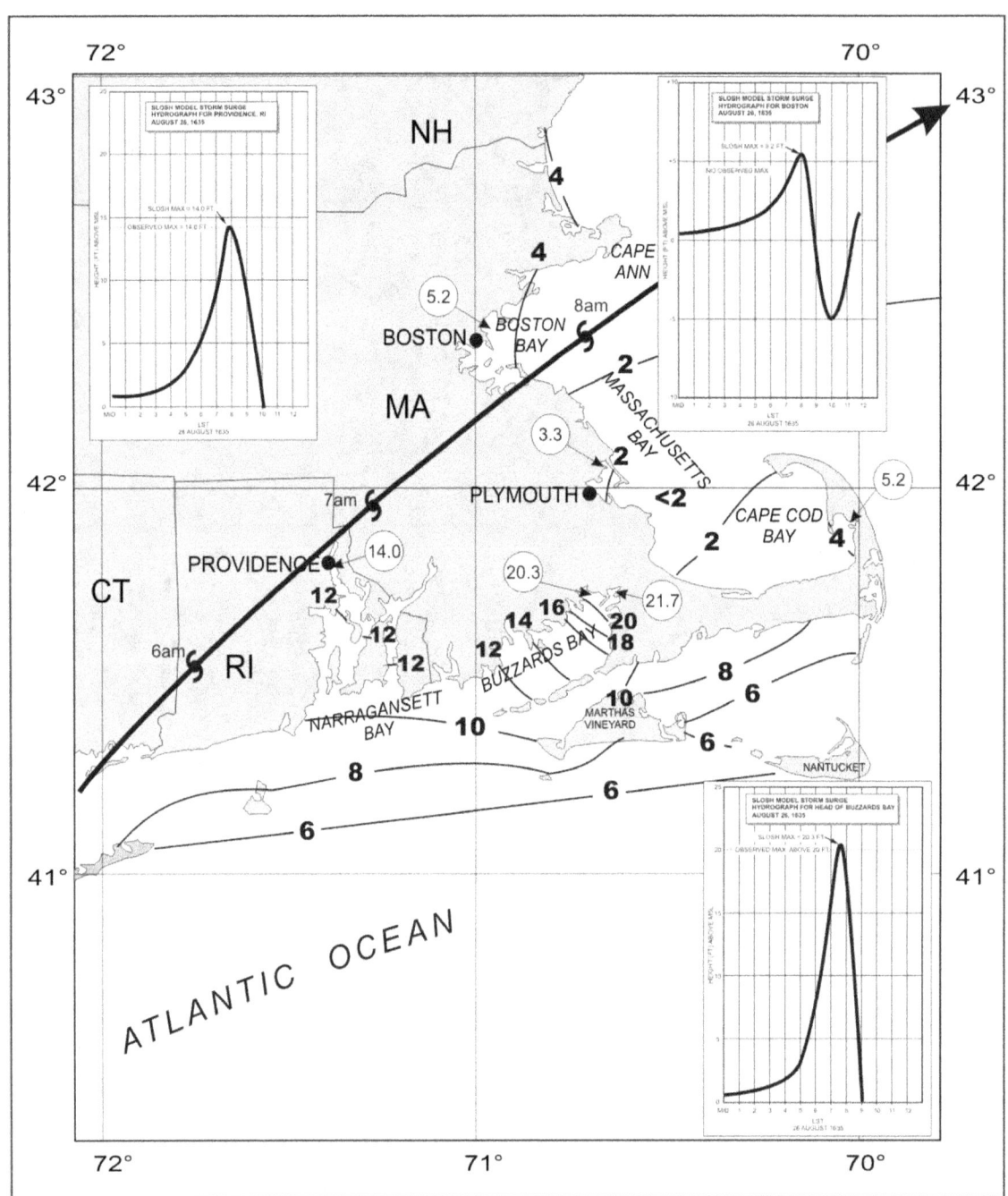

Figure 2.3 SLOSH model envelope of high water in feet above mean sea level. Contours in 2 feet increments with maximum of 14.0 feet at Providence and 21.7 feet at the head of Buzzards Bay.

SECTION 3

THE GREAT SEPTEMBER GALE OF 1815

What a difference one-hundred and eighty years makes as far as observations are concerned. Since the hurricane of 1635, the U. S. population has grown and has spread out along the coastline and inland so that when this hurricane hits, there are numerous observations that give us a good vision of the track. In addition, there are a lot of storm tide observations. Two excellent sources of information are Ludlam (1963) and Ho (1989). Ho researched many historical newspaper accounts for additional information on the hurricane before completing his analysis.

METEOROLOGICAL OBSERVATIONS

From Ludlam, "…on the morning of the 23rd. We have an ominous ship report, made at 0700 on that fatal morning when off Barnegat Inlet on the central New Jersey coast, indicating that a dead calm existed as an interim between "severe gales of great violence," first from the east-northeast and then from the west-northwest. This ship, no doubt, passed through the eye of the hurricane, when only 50 miles south of the Long Island coast."

"It was not so in New England. Rushing almost due north now at a speed close to 50 miles per hour, the great cyclonically-spinning whirl churned across Long Island Sound in a few short minutes to roar inland east of New Haven and very close to Saybrook at the mouth of the Connecticut River. The time of landfall is not known exactly- one account stated between 0800 and 0900. Our analysis would place the time very close to 0900. Both the river ports of New London and Norwich lay close to the path of the center in the dangerous eastern semicircle where forward momentum of a hurricane is added to maximum wind speeds; both places had excessive river tides as long as the winds came out of the southeast and south.

Continuing northward at undiminished speed, the eye of the vast storm crossed the plateau of eastern Connecticut and central Massachusetts, well to the east of Hartford and Springfield. The line of advance lay very close to an axis passing through Saybrook and Willimantic in Connecticut, through the Massachusetts settlements of Southbridge and Gardner, and into New Hampshire close to Jaffrey and Hillsboro. The peak of the storm passed between Amherst and Worchester in Massachusetts at approximately 1100 and thence into the hill country of New Hampshire. The editor of the *Farmer's Cabinet*, published at Amherst in New Hampshire close to Nashua and Manchester, reported: "at 1130 the severest gale of wind from the southeast ever known. The damage in this quarter is immense." The *New Hampshire Patriot's* editor at Concord presented a vivid picture of the storm in that area: "Last Saturday was experienced in this vicinity the most severe gale of wind, or rather hurricane, known by the oldest inhabitants. The wind commenced in the morning at N.E.- about noon it changed to S.E. and for two hours it seemed to threaten everything with ruin. The sturdy oak, the stately elm, and the pliant popular, were alike victims to its fury. The destruction of orchards and buildings has been great; there is scarcely an apple left on the standing trees. Many cattle have been killed by the falling trees. Had this violent wind taken place in the season of vegetation, there is no calculating its effects; It might have produced famine."

HYDROLOGIC OBSERVATIONS

In Ludlam's account of this hurricane he includes an account given by Sidney Perley who states, "At Stonington, the tide rose seventeen feet higher than usual, and swept almost entirely across the town, which is built on a tongue of land running into the water."

Also, from Perley regarding Providence, "From ten to half past eleven o'clock it blew a hurricane. About the wharves and lower part of the town generally confusion reigned. High water was about half-past eleven o'clock in the forenoon, and the wind brought in the tide ten or twelve feet above the height of the usual spring tides, and seven and a half feet higher than ever known before....".

Again from Ludlam, "At Buzzards Bay, which almost separates Cape Cod from the mainland, the peak of the winds coincided with high tide, and the waters swelled within 15 inches of covering the narrow isthmus and creating a natural canal where the Cape Cod Ship Canal later was to be dug.

In Ho's summary of the meteorological and hydrologic observations for the 1815 hurricane he identifies 15 different locations. Of these, only 6 are useful for quantitative analysis and they are listed below.

1. Bridgeport, CT: Wind shifted to NW some hours before highest tide which was observed at 12:30 pm, reaching nearly 6 feet above common flood tide.

2. Stonington, CT: Tide rose 17 feet above normal.

3. Newport, RI: Tide rose 8 feet above normal tide.

4. Warren, RI: Tide rose 7 feet higher than common spring tide.

5. Providence, RI: Wind shifted to westerly at half past eleven, tide rose 12 feet higher than spring tide.

6. New Bedford, MA: Tide rose about 10 feet above high water mark (or 12 to 14 feet higher than usual)

So Providence, Rhode Island, has two observations from two different sources, observation number 5 above and the 10 to 12 feet from Perley's account in Ludlam. I decided to use 11.0 feet for the observed.

The water elevations at these 6 locations were first adjusted to mean sea level. In all six cases we assumed that the observer was referencing the height of the water above normal or common tide or spring tide. The elevation of the normal or spring tide above mean sea level is approximately known at each location. For example, at Warren, RI the height of the common spring tide is 3.2 feet msl. Thus, the height of the storm tide at Warren was 10.2 feet msl. The value for Warren and the other locations are shown in Table 3.1 in the second column.

Table 3.1

Location (ft msl)	SLOSH/TIDE (ft msl)	Observed (ft msl)	SLOSH/TIDE -Observed (ft)
Bridgeport, CT	9.3	9.2	0.1
Stonington, CT	8.3	18.2 (8.2)	-9.9 (0.1)
Newport, RI	9.7	10.0	-0.3
Warren, RI	10.6	10.2	0.4
Providence, RI	13.8	14.4	-0.6
New Bedford, MA	12.2	11.8	0.4

These values are the ones we want to obtain a "best fit for" when they are compared to the maximum values calculated from the sum of the SLOSH and tide model hydrographs.

First, however, we need a preliminary track, intensity and RMW for the SLOSH model.

DISCUSSION

Both Ludlam and Ho are in relative accord on the track of the hurricane. They disagree on the speed based on decisions made for the times they assigned to their respective landfall positions in Connecticut. After analyzing all the available data, my track is closest to Ludlam's track. I have made the landfall time at Saybrook, CT a little after 9 am on the 23rd of September. The noon position should be a little northwest of Concord, NH based upon the account mentioned earlier. The distance traveled by the hurricane in 3 hours is approximately 150 miles (or 50 mph). By extrapolating the track southward into the Atlantic, the 7 am position would approximately agree with the ship observation. (Note: The ship position was unknown but was probably "abeam" of Barnegat Inlet.) The extrapolation was completed in both directions and the final track with the hourly values is shown in Figure 3.1.

SLOSH MODEL SIMULATIONS

As was done for the 1635 hurricane a series of SLOSH model runs were made with the track shown on Figure 3.1. The central pressure and RMW were varied until it was in agreement with the storm surge observations. However, it immediately became apparent that the value at Stonington, CT was incorrect and it was removed and the iteration process continued. This observation will be discussed later. Figure 3.2 shows the best fit track across Long Island and New England. The hourly values in local standard time are plotted along with the central pressure. Near landfall in Connecticut, the SLOSH model calculated a maximum one-minute wind over water of 122 mph. It is shown as a wind vector that is plotted at the radius of maximum winds which is 30 st. mi. The location of the maximum winds at a particular time are shown as circles in the figure. Maximum wind vectors are also plotted at Providence, Boston and Bridgeport. These three locations would likely have recorded lower sustained one-minute speeds because the computation of the SLOSH winds assumes unrestricted flow on the water surface at the location. At all three of these locations the wind was "restricted" because of interaction with land and vegetation. However, the qualitative descriptions by the observers at the various locations can be compared to the SLOSH wind profile to assess the validity of the timing of the events.

The hurricane was probably a category 4 hurricane, as it passed by the Outer Banks of North Carolina. It was likely interacting with a major trough located to the west which was accelerating it toward the north and later north-northeast. It probably began filling just north of Cape Hatteras where the sea surface temperatures begin decreasing in late September. The hurricane made landfall on Long Island with a sea level pressure of 956 mb and a second landfall in Connecticut with a pressure of 957 mb. The hurricane was moving north-northeast about 50 mph and had a RMW of approximately 30 st. mi.

Two examples of how the final storm tide value was determined for each location is given for Providence, RI and Bridgeport, CT, and is shown in Figure 3.3. First the SLOSH model hydrograph was plotted relative to msl. Next the hindcast of the tide hydrograph was plotted relative to msl. The two hydrographs were added together to get the storm tide hydrograph. The maximum value from the storm tide hydrograph was compared to the observed maximum storm tide. The SLOSH/TIDE computed values for the 6 locations are shown in the first column of Table1. The third column is the difference. Also, shown in Figure 3.3, for each location, is a SLOSH model wind speed profile in miles per hour and a direction barb to indicate the direction from which the wind is blowing.

Overall the results are good except for Stonington, CT, as mentioned above. This is a common problem in dealing with high water marks and about 1-2 percent of observations are inconsistent with the model results by a large margin. It is likely caused by one of two reasons. First, it could be a combination of storm tide and breaking wave height in a structure or secondly, there could have been an error in the report. If the number one is removed from the 18.2 feet then you have 8.2 feet which agrees quite well with the computed value and also fits better with its neighboring observed values.

How do the results in Figure 3.3 compare to descriptions by observers at these locations? At Providence, "From ten to half past eleven it blew a hurricane." The SLOSH wind profile shows a southerly wind at 115 mph at 10 am increasing to 117 mph about ten minutes later and decreasing to 82 mph at half past eleven. "High water was about half past eleven o'clock in the forenoon, and the wind brought in the tide ten or twelve feet above the height of the usual spring tides...". The SLOSH/TIDE hydrograph shows the maximum occurring at 1210 or about 40 minutes after observed and it is about 12 feet higher than the tide. At Bridgeport, "The late storm, which commenced on Thursday with increasing violence until 11 o'clock...That the tide which in ordinary weather would have been full at 2 o'clock and 44 minutes, attained its greatest height at 12 o'clock 30 minutes, and was then near six feet above common flood tides, and had it not fortunately happened that the wind some hours before the tide was full veered round to the N.W. it must have risen to an alarming height." The SLOSH wind profile shows increasing winds up to about 930 to 1000 or about one hour short of the observation. However, the wind does turn and blows from the northwest some hours before the storm tide was full or reached its maximum. The SLOSH/TIDE hydrograph shows a maximum at about 1210 versus 1230 observed.

SLOSH/TIDE hydrographs for other locations were computed and the maximums are discussed in light of any qualitative observations.

At the Head of Buzzards Bay the maximum is 15.9 feet msl. The description of the observed height of the storm tide at this location is that it was 15 inches below the isthmus that separates Buzzards Bay from Cape Cod Bay. This is an interesting observation in that the 1635 hurricane storm tide must have topped the isthmus and sent water into Cape Cod Bay. So what is the height of the isthmus? In 1776 George Washington sent an engineering team to determine the feasibility of constructing a canal there, hoping to thwart a British blockade. At this writing a search is ongoing to find the original 1776 detailed engineering survey created by this team. If the height of the isthmus can be determined then a comparison can be made.

At Boston the maximum is 3.5 feet msl. The SLOSH model shows a storm surge maximum of 2.8 feet, but it occurs near mean tide. The maximum high tide at Boston is almost 5.0 feet msl so that no water exceeded the maximum tide height. The account at Boston says nothing about excessive water and only talks about the strong winds.

At Nantucket Island the maximum was 3.5 feet or about 1.8 feet above the high tide mark and the SLOSH model one-minute wind speed maximum was 60 mph. The observation there was, "In Nantucket very little injury was experienced from the wind and the tide was not unusually high."

SUMMARY FOR THE 1815 HURRICANE

The 1815 hurricane was a category 3 on the Saffir/Simpson scale. The central pressure was 956 mb at landfall on Long Island and 957 mb at landfall in Connecticut. The storm was moving about 50 mph with a radius of maximum winds of 30 st. mi. Maximum one-minute winds at landfall were calculated at 122 mph. Maximum observed storm tides in feet relative to mean sea level were available for 5 locations, with the highest being at Providence (14.4 feet). The highest storm tide calculated by SLOSH/TIDE model is at the head of Buzzards Bay (15.9 feet).

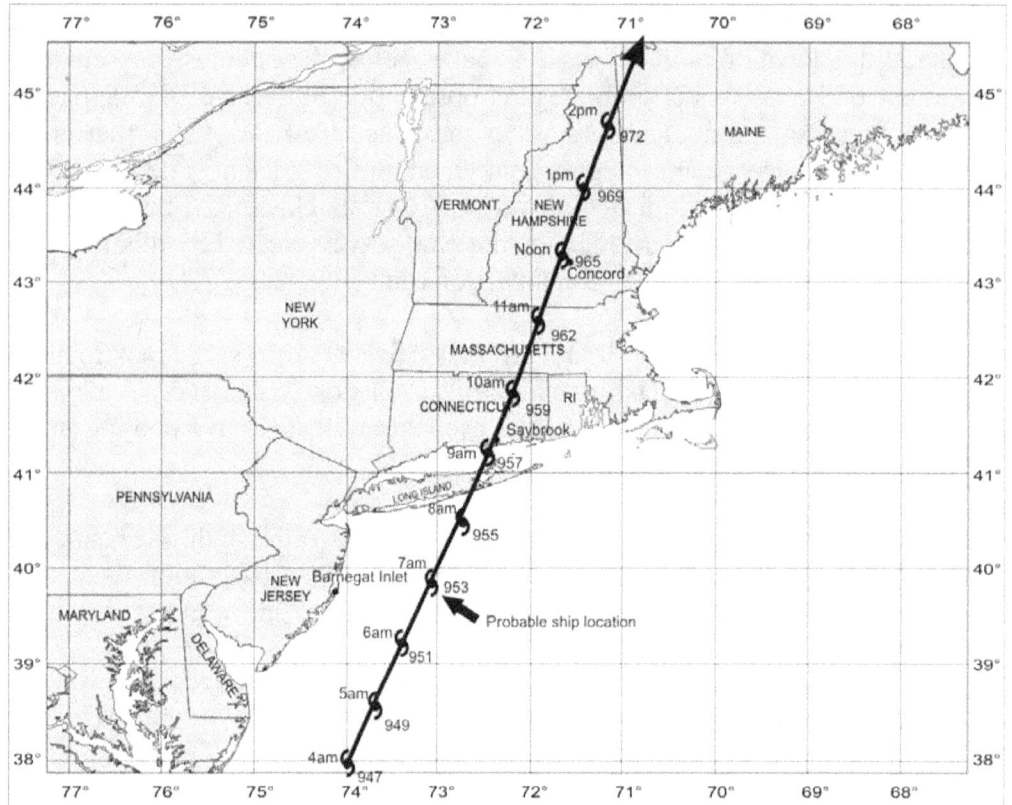

Figure 3.1 Track of the Great September Gale on September 23, 1815, with hourly positions in local standard time and central pressure in millibars.

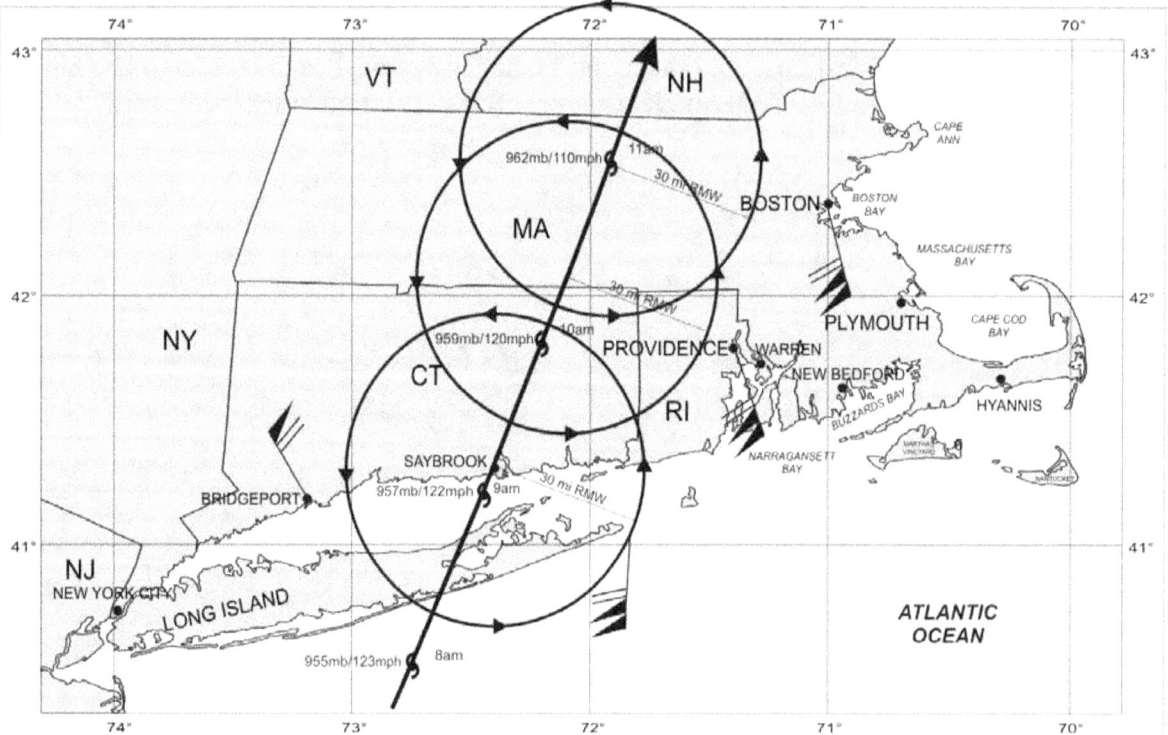

Figure 3.2 Track of the September 23, 1815 hurricane with hourly positions in local standard time, pressure in millibars and SLOSH model maximum over water 1-minute wind speed in miles per hour. Circles represent location of maximum wind with radius given in statute miles. Wind vectors show where maximum wind is occurring at that time. Wind barbs in mph.

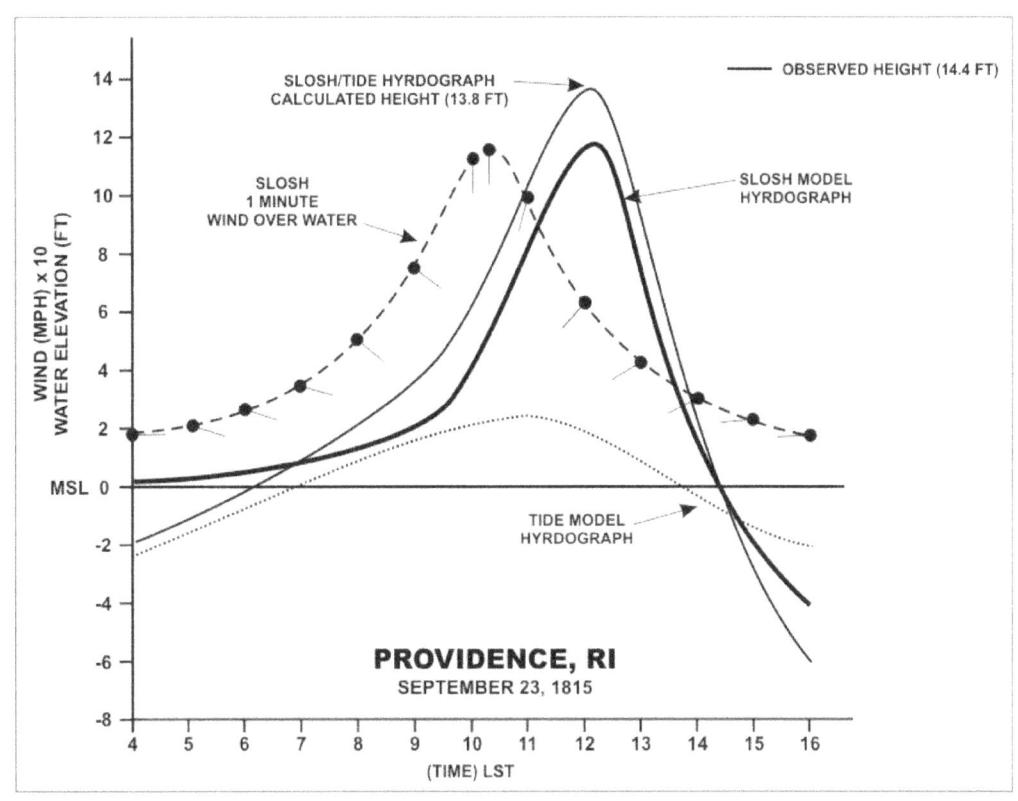

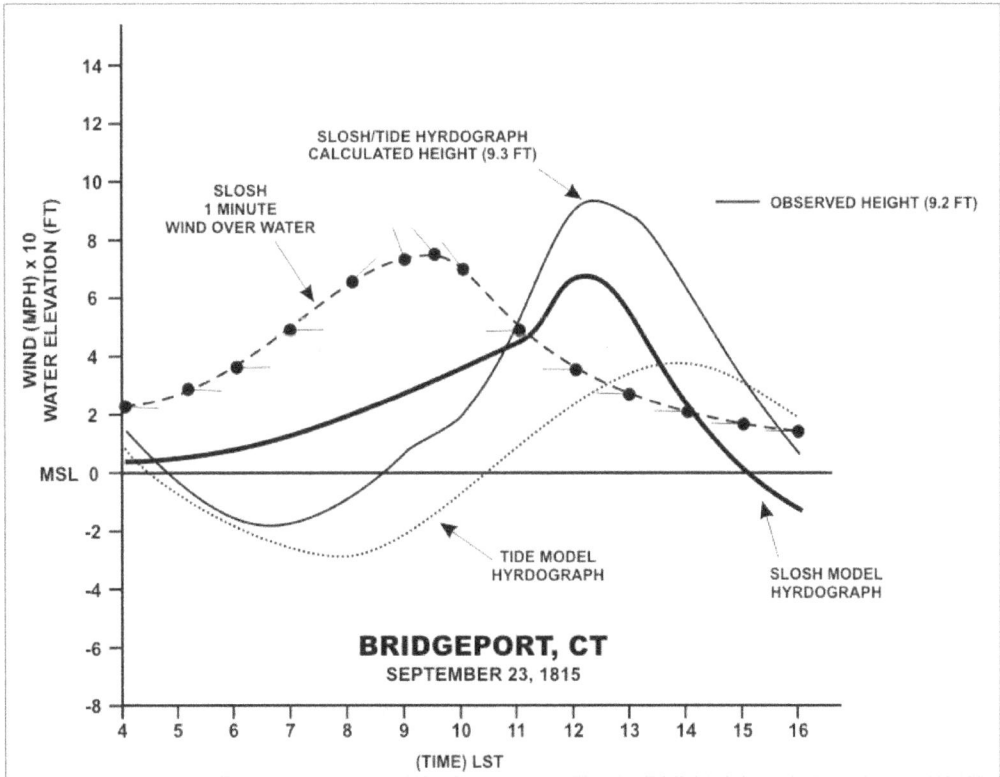

Figure 3.3 Graphical computation of the storm tide hydrograph from the addition of the SLOSH and tide hydrographs at two locations. The peak of the storm tide hydrograph is compared to the observed height. SLOSH model over water 1-minute wind speeds in miles per hour are plotted with wind barbs indicating direction.

SECTION 4

THE 1938 NEW ENGLAND HURRICANE

INTRODUCTION

One-hundred and twenty three years had passed since the 1815 hurricane. The coastal population had been steadily growing since 1815 and had developed many seaside weekend and summer getaways as well as permanent homes along the New England shorelines. Thus, there are more recorded visual accounts of this hurricane than any previous storms. Also and probably more important, there were scientific instruments available to measure the atmosphere as well as the water level. Many locations were remote and/or at low-lying elevations which proved to be disastrous for many people. The 1938 hurricane is the standard by which all others are measured in the northeast. Many articles have been written and television documentaries made about this hurricane. Extensive photo galleries by different individuals and groups easily show the massive destruction wrought by this hurricane. Before and after photographs document the combined destructive forces of the storm tide and the breaking waves. A few photos show the rising water as it occurred but were generally taken well inland from the coast. Although warnings were issued for this hurricane, there was great difficulty in disseminating them. Its rapid acceleration northward left many people vulnerable to the storm surge and breaking waves. Over 600 people perished, mostly due to drowning. Surprisingly, many individuals who were forced into the storm tide and breaking waves have left incredible accounts of their struggles and survival.

METEOROLOGICAL DATA

In the year that followed this hurricane, there were numerous meteorological journal articles published. Each one contained some useful information. Tannehill (1938) listed and commented on some of the observations available immediately after the hurricane. Pierce (1939) gave an excellent history of the hurricane including hourly surface pressure analyses and information about the upper level winds at six and ten thousand feet. Wexler (1939) discussed the filling of the hurricane after landfall. The most comprehensive analysis was done by Myers and Jordan (1956). They had additional ship information that was not available at the time of Pierce's study. Their track and their pressure values were used for the SLOSH model run. Minor adjustments were made to their track to obtain uniform hourly acceleration/deceleration values.

HYDROLOGIC DATA

The post high water mark survey and tide gage data is well documented in Harris (1963). Although the process of obtaining surveyed high water marks had been done in several hurricanes prior to this one, this was the first extensive high water mark survey done in the U.S. Most of the high water marks were collected by the U. S. Army Corps of Engineers with additional ones supplied by Woods Hole Oceanographic Institution and others. In many cases, elevations were collected within one-half mile or less of each other. This resulted in hundreds of marks available for verification. The surveyed area included the coastal areas of northern New Jersey, New York (including all of Long Island), Connecticut, Rhode Island and southern Massachusetts. It is beyond the scope of this paper to verify each high water mark against a SLOSH/TIDE generated value. However, verification will take place at the locations that were done in the 1635 and 1815 hurricanes. Even more valuable than the high water marks are the observed storm tide hydrographs at many tide gage locations. Harris not only reported on these gages but also removed the astronomical tide from the storm tide hydrograph to reveal a storm surge hydrograph which can be compared directly with the SLOSH model hydrograph. Unfortunately, in 1938 their were no tide gages in Narragansett Bay and the Woods Hole tide gage in Buzzards Bay failed.

DISCUSSION

According to Myers and Jordan the hurricane began to rapidly accelerate northward just east of the Outer Banks of North Carolina and reached a maximum forward speed of approximately 70 miles per hour around 11 am on September 21. The hurricane then began to decelerate and was moving at around 40 miles per hour at landfall on Long Island at around 3 pm and 38 miles per hours at landfall in Connecticut less then an hour later. Subsequently, the surface pressure data then supported a rapid jump forward from 5 to 6 pm before the hurricane began to slow again in upstate New York. The track of the hurricane with hourly positions and pressure in millibars is shown in Figure 4.1. From surface wind observations taken near the eye, Myers and Jordon determined that the RMW in front of the hurricane ranged from 50 to 57 statute miles and behind the eye, from 35 to 40 statute miles. The one parameter that Myers and Jordan had a problem with was the RMW on the east side of the hurricane because of lack of wind data. They concluded that it was west of Block Island which recorded the highest winds east of the center and estimated the RMW at 57 statute miles. Another estimate of the RMW can be determined from the width of the reported calm winds, which was approximately 50 statute miles and was roughly centered on Bellport. Note that the wind center appears to be located to the southwest of the pressure center as pointed out in the article by Myers and Jordan. This explains why Hartford had a lower pressure than New Haven, but Hartford did not experience a calm as New Haven did. Thus, the preliminary radius of maximum winds (RMW) could be approximately 25 plus 5 statute miles or 30 statute miles. The 5 statute miles allows the winds to increase from calm to the maximum value. The RMW could be anywhere in the range 30 to 57 statute miles. From the SLOSH model simulations it was determined to be 30 statute miles from the pressure center. If the actual wind center observed in the hurricane was used, the value would be approximately 40 to 45 statute miles. Figure 4.2 shows the track of the hurricane through the northeast. At selected times the location of the maximum winds is represented by the circle with a 30 statute miles radius. The maximum SLOSH calculated over the water 1-minute wind speed in miles per hour is depicted by a wind vector. Also shown are the sites where a minimum pressure was recorded and the time that it occurred. For example, the minimum pressure at the Bellport Coast Guard Station was 946 millibars at 2:45 pm; New Haven, 952 millibars at 3:50 pm and Hartford, 949 millibars at 4:30 pm. The hurricane made its first landfall on the south shore of Long Island with a pressure of 941 millibars at about 2:45 pm. It then made a second landfall on the coast of Connecticut with a pressure of 946 millibars at about 3:40 pm.

Storm tide high water marks along the Rhode Island and southern Massachusetts shoreline ranged from 5.1 to 15.8 feet. The highest value of 15.8 feet occurred at Providence at the head of Narragansett Bay. The next highest values occurred at the Head of Buzzards Bay and were in the range 14.0 to 14.5 feet. The values at the mouth of Narragansett Bay ranged from 10 to 12 feet. The coast of Connecticut had values ranging from 9.1 to 11.5 feet and the largest values were located along the western Connecticut shoreline. On the north coast of Long Island the values ranged from 7.2 to approximately 13.0 feet. Again, the highest values were at the western end of the island. Several high water marks were recorded higher then 13.0 feet but seem to have additional height in them due to breaking waves. This is even more apparent along the south shore of Long Island where many values appear to have a breaking wave component in the value. For example, a high water value recorded at the eastern tip of Long Island near Montauk Point was 15.7 feet. The water is deep near this location and this factor causes lower storm surge and/or storm tide heights compared to shallower locations. However, it is ideal for large waves to get close before they break and run-up on the shoreline. Values of 6 to 7 feet would be more likely for the 1938 hurricane at this location. Farther west on the south coast, the values ranged from 10 to 12 feet on the barrier islands and 3 to 7 feet in the bays. Raritan Bay, Lower and Upper New York Harbor and the Hudson River had values that ranged from 4 to 8 feet.

SLOSH MODEL SIMULATION

The SLOSH model zero datum is NGVD. By the time of 1938 hurricane, sea level had risen about 0.1 feet above NGVD. Thus, 0.1 feet of water was added to all of the SLOSH grid cells that represent water. This is called the initial height. A SLOSH model simulation was made with the track information shown in Figures 4.1 and 4.2. Similar to the 1815 hurricane, SLOSH model and Tide model hydrographs were created and added together to produce storm tide hydrographs at Providence and the head of Buzzards Bay. These are shown in Figure 4.3 and are compared to the values shown in Harris. In both locations the comparisons are within several tenths of a foot. The hydrographs for Providence show that the maximum storm surge arrived near high tide creating a worst case scenario. However, at the head of Buzzards Bay the maximum storm surge arrived just before high tide. If it had also arrived at high tide, an additional 0.6 to 0.7 feet would have occurred. At New Haven the maximum storm surge arrived near or just after mean tide so the high water mark as reported by Harris at that location is primarily due to storm surge and can be compared directly to the SLOSH model value. The observed value was 9.3 feet and SLOSH was 10.3 feet.

The SLOSH model maximum 1-minute over water wind was 130 miles per hour at the southern shoreline on eastern Long Island and 120 miles per hour at the shoreline in eastern Connecticut. Block Island which was located east of the maximum winds reported a maximum 10-minute sustained wind of 91 miles per hour with a gust to 121 miles per hour. The SLOSH model wind 1-minute wind for Block Island was 106 miles per hour. With modern wind measuring devices, relationships have been established between the different time averaged wind speeds. For example, the10-minute wind can be converted to a 1-minute wind by multiplying by 1.12, giving a 12 percent difference. If this relationship holds for the wind measuring device at Block Island during the 1938 hurricane then we can convert the 10-minute wind to a 1-minute wind. Multiplying 91 miles per hour by 1.12 gives 102 miles per hour, which is 3 to 4 percent less than the SLOSH value. The next hurricane to be investigated is hurricane Carol in 1954. This wind comparison will be done again at Block Island for Carol.

SUMMARY FOR THE 1938 HURRICANE

The 1938 hurricane was a category 3.5 hurricane on the Saffir/Simpson hurricane scale at landfall on Long Island. The central pressure was 941 millibars at landfall on eastern Long Island and 946 millibars at landfall on the coast of Connecticut. The hurricane was decelerating as it approached land and was moving at approximately 40 miles per hour at landfall on Long Island and 38 miles per hour at landfall in Connecticut. The RMW was 30 statute miles on the east side of the hurricane, when measured from the pressure center, and was the value used for the SLOSH simulation in this study. The RMW was larger when measured from the wind center which was located about 14 miles southwest of the pressure center as determined by Myers and Jordan. SLOSH/Tide model storm tide elevations at Providence (16.1 feet) and the head of Buzzard Bay (13.8 feet) agree quite well with the observed values of 15.8 and 14.1 feet respectively.

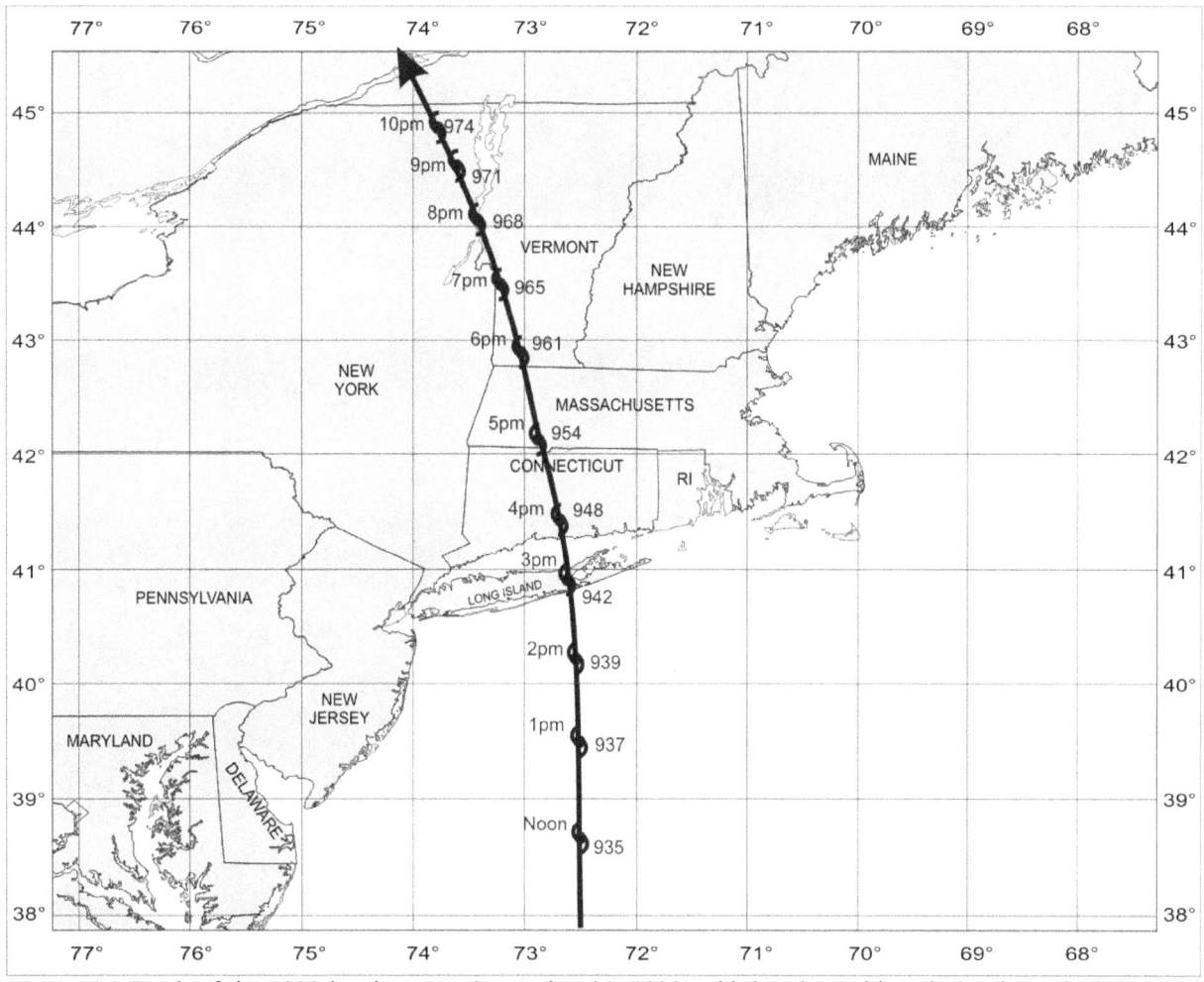

Figure 4.1 Track of the 1938 hurricane on September 21, 1938, with hourly positions in local standard time and central pressure in millibars.

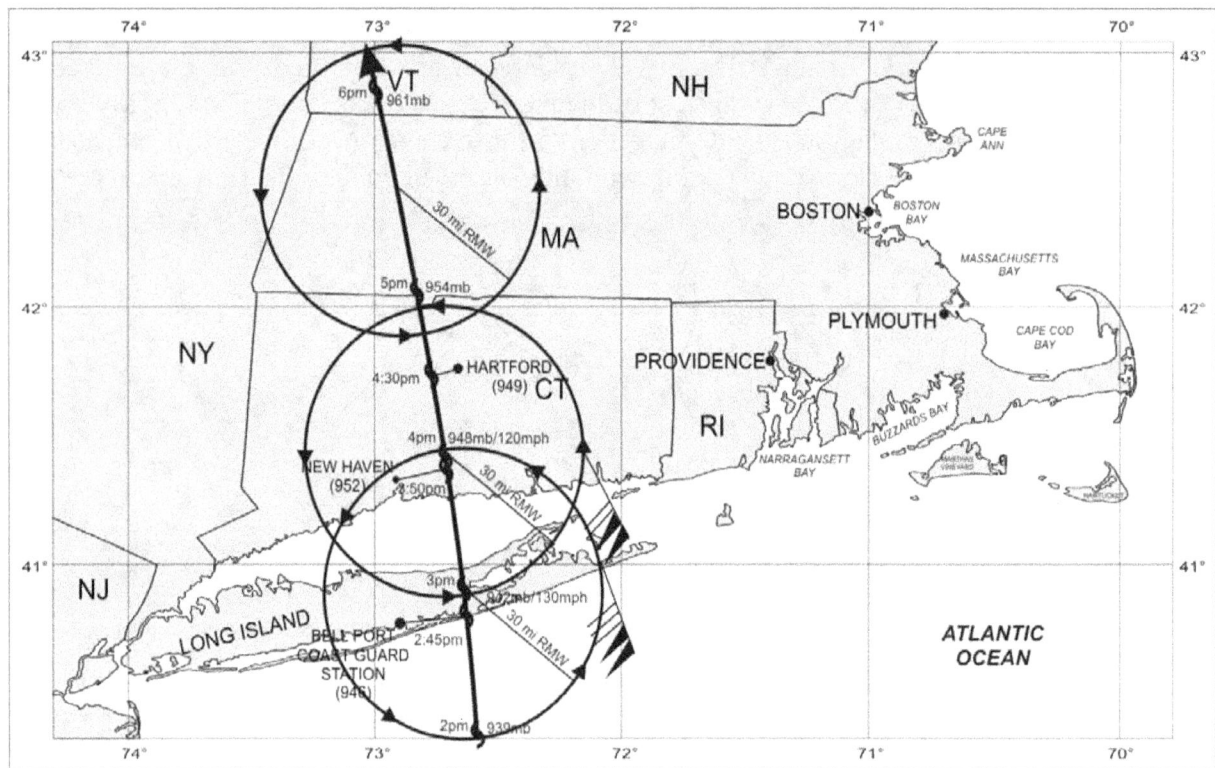

Figure 4.2 Track of the September 21, 1938 hurricane with hourly positions in local standard time, pressure in millibars and SLOSH model maximum over water 1-minute wind speed in miles per hour. Circles represent location of maximum wind with radius given in statute miles. Wind vectors show where maximum wind is occurring at that time. Wind barbs in mph.

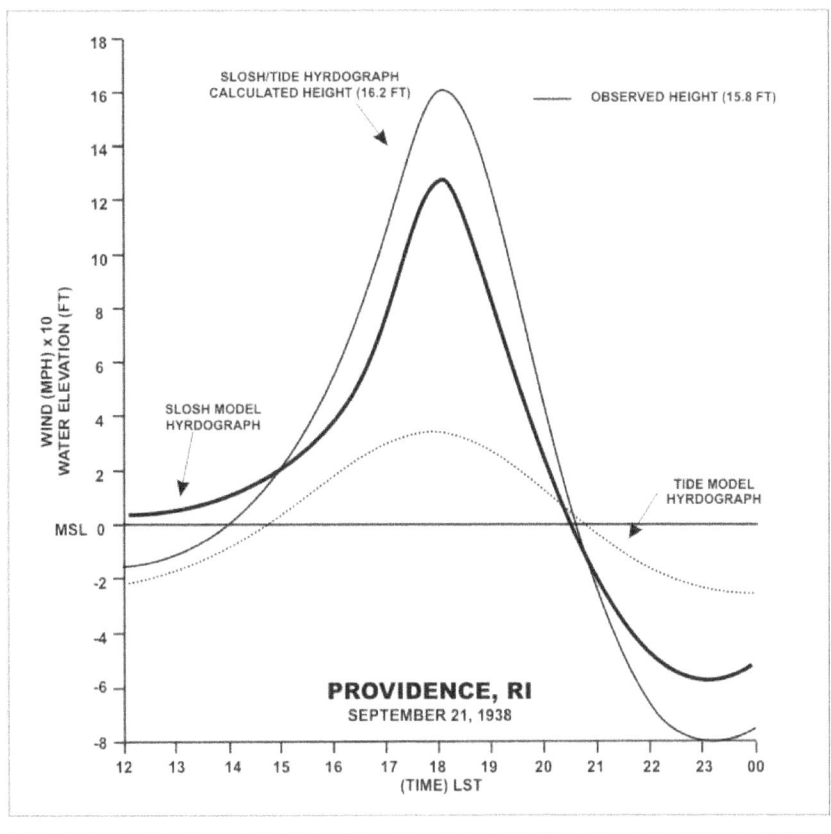

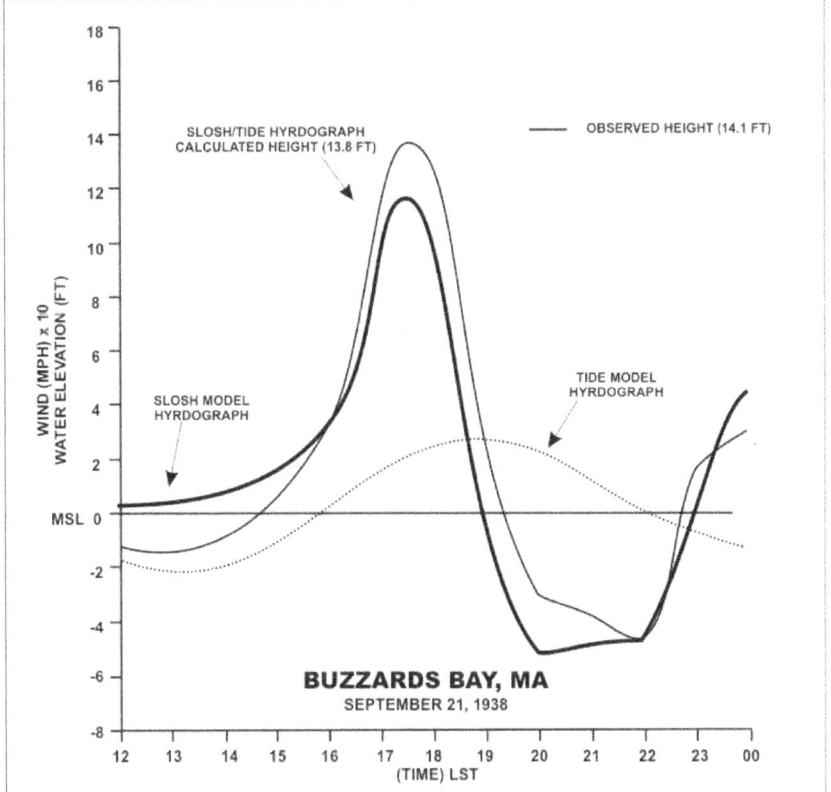

Figure 4.3 Graphical computation of the storm tide hydrograph from the addition of the SLOSH and tide hydrographs at two locations. The peak of the storm tide hydrograph is compared to the observed height.

SECTION 5

HURRICANE CAROL (1954)

Hurricane reconnaissance is now an important tool and the observations it generates helps to determine the location, intensity, size and speed of translation just before landfall in New England. Also, there is a wealth of high water mark data and tide gage hydrographs.

METEOROLOGICAL DATA

A hurricane season summary article by Davis (1954) offers very little information on this hurricane especially at landfall in New England. Additional articles by Rhodes (1954) and McGuire (1954) add some additional information. From the above sources and the Navy hurricane reconnaissance log on August 31, we know the following:

1. The recon made a center fix from a 500 foot altitude at 8:37 am and reported an extrapolated pressure of 964 millibars. It also reported a maximum flight level and surface wind blowing from the west (270 degrees) at 115 miles per hour located 40 nautical miles south-southwest of the center. The radar presentation showed an elliptical shaped eye with the north to south axis measuring 45 nautical miles and the east to west axis measuring 33 nautical miles.
2. The eye passed over Groton, CT at about 10:00 am on the 31st of August. The sky cleared and the winds dropped and a rapid increase in the winds to hurricane force occurred 30 minutes later. The lowest pressure recorded at the Coast Guard Moorings Station was 957 millibars.
3. The lowest pressure recorded at the Suffolk County Airport on Long Island was 960 millibars. Other values were 965 millibars at Block Island and 972 millibars at Quonset Airport in North Kingstown, RI.
4. Surface pressure data and subsequent analyses were available after Carol passed inland into New England and these center positions were utilized in the track construction.
5. Reported maximum sustained wind speeds/with gusts in miles per hour were 100/135 at Block Island, NY; 90/105 at Warwick, RI. ; 90/115 at the Green State Airport near Narragansett, RI.

HYDROLOGIC DATA

Similar to what took place after the 1938 hurricane, an extensive high water mark survey was conducted and the results summarized in Harris (1963). Comparison of the hundreds of high water marks to SLOSH/TIDE model values is beyond the scope of this paper. Thus, only two, one in Providence and the other at the head of Buzzards Bay were selected for comparison. Also, Harris produced storm surge hydrographs by removing the tide from the tide gage records and plotted them. The SLOSH model maximum was compared to the maximum from the Harris produced hydrographs at five locations.

DISCUSSION

The track of hurricane Carol with hourly positions in local standard time and lowest sea level pressure in millibars is shown in figure 5.1. The center fix by the reconnaissance aircraft is denoted by a triangle. After the hurricane passed over the Outer Banks of North Carolina, it accelerated toward the north-northeast. Based upon the center fix and points inland, the maximum translational speed of 47 mph occurred around 9 to 10 am just before the first landfall on eastern Long Island with a pressure of 956 millibars. A short time later it made a second landfall and passed over Groton, CT with a pressure of 957 millibars when it began to slow down. The center passed about 35 miles to the west of Boston, MA, near noon with an estimated pressure of 962 to 963 millibars. This low pressure and subsequent pressure gradient caused very strong winds and wind gusts over eastern Massachusetts and caused one of the noted landmarks in Boston to be damaged. The steeple of the Old North Church, after standing since 1806 (146 years), was blown down and crashed into the street. The reconnaissance pressure seemed to be high based upon the surface observations. A pressure gradient analysis based upon the track passing over Groton supports the 957 millibars at this location. A perpendicular distance from the track to the 960 millibars at the Suffolk County Airport is about 16 statute miles toward the west-northwest. Analyzing the reconnaissance data, including the elliptical shape of the eye, as well as the pressure and surface wind reports near landfall, the RMW was determined to be approximately 25 st mi. Figure 5.2 shows the hourly track and pressure values across New England. Also shown, at selected times, are a series of circles representing the location of the maximum winds. The radial distance of 25 statute miles is also shown. It is obvious that the winds on the east side of the hurricane are driving water up Narragansett Bay which resulted in the highest water elevations at the head of the bay. Also, Boston would have experienced strong winds on the east side of the center. Plotted in several locations on these circles are wind vectors showing the maximum one-minute wind speed calculated by the SLOSH model over water.

SLOSH MODEL SIMULATION

The SLOSH model zero datum is NGVD. By the time of Carol's occurrence sea level had risen about 0.3 feet above NGVD. Thus, 0.3 feet of water was added to all of the SLOSH grid cells that represent water. This is called the initial height. A SLOSH model simulation was made with this initial height and the meteorological input data shown in the figures. The comparison of the results to observed tide gage storm surge maximums, determined by Harris, is shown in Table 5.1. Note: The values at Providence and the head of Buzzards Bay are storm tide high water marks. SLOSH/TIDE model heights were determined at these locations for comparisons.

Table 5.1

Location (ft msl)	SLOSH/TIDE (ft msl)	Observed (ft msl)	SLOSH/TIDE -Observed (ft)
Providence	14.6	14.8*	-0.2
Head of Buzzards Bay	16.4	13.4*	3.0
Newport	8.1	8.2	-0.1
Woods Hole	8.2	8.0	0.2
New London	10.2	6.8	3.4
Montauk Point	5.6	6.1	-0.5
Boston	3.9	3.6	0.3

* Denotes high water mark and represents storm tide

Overall the differences are typical, except the SLOSH model is high at New London and at the head of Buzzards Bay.

SUMMARY FOR HURRICANE CAROL

Hurricane Carol was a category 3 hurricane when it made landfall in New England. One observer commented that it was a true hurricane in that there were no fronts wrapped into it. The size at landfall seems to support this statement in that it had the smallest RMW of the four hurricanes investigated in the northeast. Also, its arrival on the last day of August, when the sea surface temperatures are near their maximum values, certainly played a role in maintaining its hurricane characteristics.

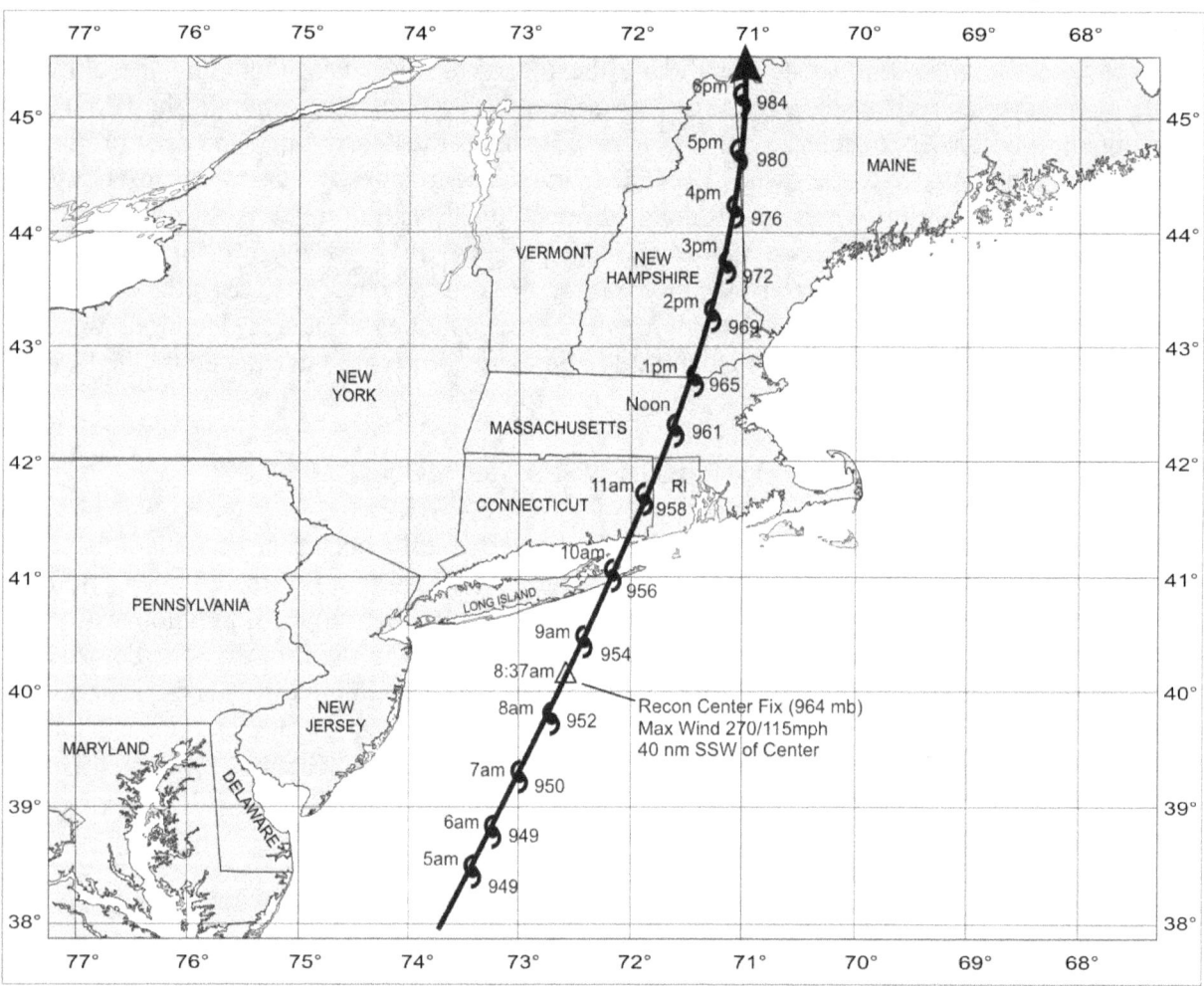

Figure 5.1 Track of hurricane Carol, August 31, 1954, with hourly positions in local standard time and central pressure in millibars.

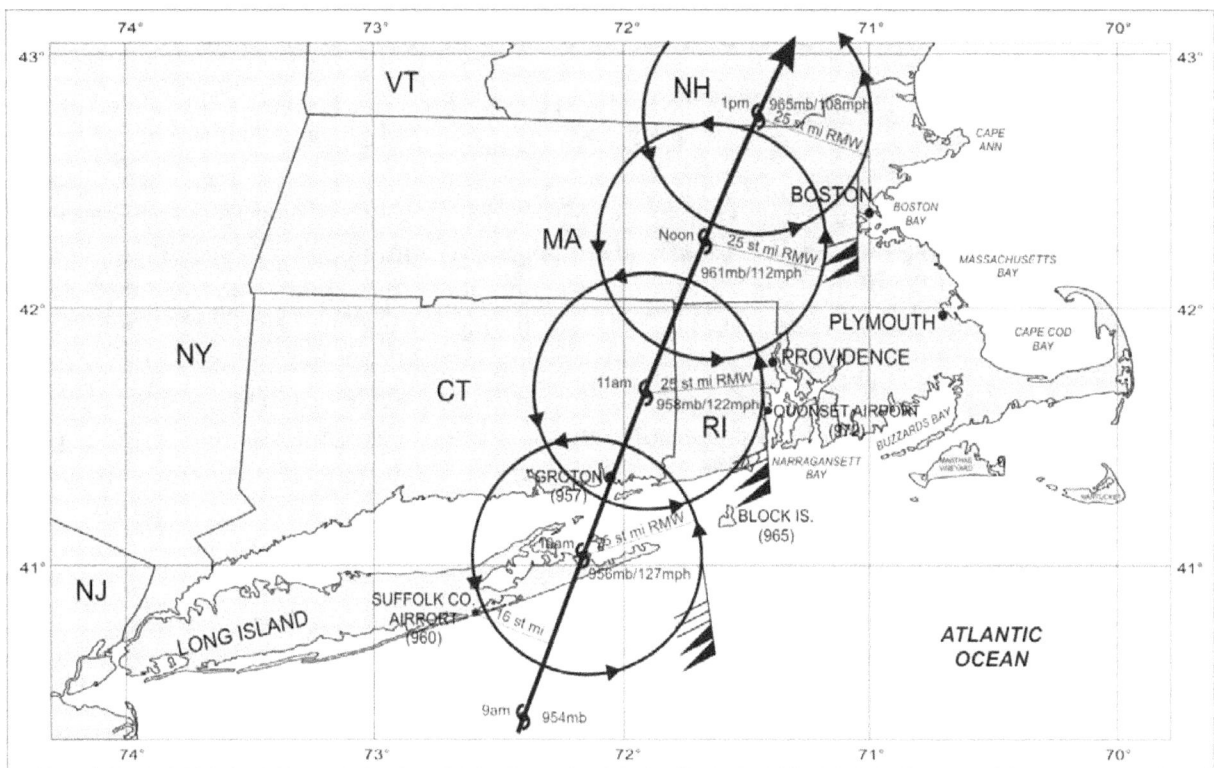

Figure 5.2 Track of hurricane Carol, August 31, 1954, with hourly positions in local standard time, pressure in millibars and SLOSH model maximum over water 1-minute wind speed in miles per hour. Circles represent location of maximum wind with radius given in statute miles. Wind vectors show where maximum wind is occurring at that time. Wind barbs in mph.

SECTION 6

COMPARISON OF FOUR INTENSE HURRICANES THAT AFFECTED NEW ENGLAND

A comparison will be made of the hurricanes in 1635, 1815, 1938 and Carol (1954). The values to be compared are the sea level pressure, the maximum 1-minute wind speed, the RMW, translation speed and direction at landfall on Long Island and Connecticut, and the storm tide at Providence and at the head of Buzzards Bay. The storm tide for the 1635 hurricane could not be determined because no tide hindcast model for this time period was available. At Providence and the head of Buzzards Bay the range for the storm tide can be determined approximately by adding/subtracting one-half of the average tide range to/from the observed storm surge. For this hurricane the original observations which represent storm surge, were used. Table 6.1 shows the comparisons.

The values can be ranked in order of intensity. Ranked by pressure in millibars, the 1635 is first with 938 millibars, 1938 is second with 941, Carol is third with 955 and 1815 is last with 956. Ordering by wind speed in miles per hour, the 1635 and 1938 are the same at 132 miles per hour, followed by Carol with 130 and the 1815 with 122. The 1635 hurricane had the largest Radius of Maximum Winds (RMW) at 35 statute miles followed by both the 1815 and 1938 hurricanes at 30 statute miles and Carol at 25 statute miles. Carol's small RMW and fast forward speed is the reason for the high maximum wind speed which is comparable to the wind speeds in both the 1635 and 1938 hurricanes. While the 1938 hurricane has had a historical reputation of being a fast moving hurricane, in reality it was one of the slowest at landfall. It had reached a top forward speed of 70 miles per hour well south of Long Island but was decelerating as it made landfall. The size of the RMWs on the right sides of these hurricanes is somewhat surprising since some more recent hurricanes of lesser intensities had larger RMWs. However, this may be the point, that is- the only way to have an intense hurricane in the northeastern U.S. is with a smaller size RMW. The most likely months are August and September when the sea surface temperatures are the warmest. Late August is generally the time when the peak sea surface temperatures occur at these latitudes.

All of the maximum 1-minute over the water wind values were taken from the SLOSH model. In the comparison of the SLOSH maximum 1-minute winds to the observed maximum wind at Block Island for the 1938 hurricane and hurricane Carol in 1954 the SLOSH model winds were higher than the observed by 3 to 4 percent and 12 to 13 percent respectively. However, some of this difference can be explained by the effects of the friction of the island's terrain which reduced the speed of the actual winds. It is likely that the SLOSH model winds are within about 5 percent of the observed winds when the observation site has a good marine exposure.

At Providence, the maximum historical storm tide of 15.8 feet occurred in the 1938 hurricane. However, it could become second highest because the 1635 hurricane could have a storm tide in the range from approximately 11.5 to 17.5 feet depending on the stage of the tide which is unknown at this time. Hurricane Carol is next at 14.8 feet followed by the 1815 hurricane at 14.4 feet. At the head of Buzzards Bay, the maximum is the 1635 hurricane. Its exact value is not known but the range of the storm tide could be approximately 18.0 to 24 feet. This greatly exceeds the other values of 15.9 feet in the 1815 hurricane, 14.1 feet in the 1938 hurricane and 13.4 feet in Carol.

An effort was made to determine only the storm surge maximums at these two locations. The results are interesting and show how important the interaction with the tide is in producing the storm tide. At Providence, Carol produced the maximum storm surge of 14.5 feet. In Carol, the peak surge arrived near mean tide. Had it arrived 3 hours later, the storm tide would have been near 18 feet and would have held the record for high storm tide of these four storms. The next is the 1635 hurricane at 14.0 feet followed by the 1938 at 12.8 feet and 1815 at 11.8 feet. As in many endeavors, including storm tide, timing is everything! At the head of Buzzards Bay without a doubt the record is the 1635 hurricane at greater than 20 feet followed by the 1815 hurricane at 13.7 feet, Carol and the 1938 hurricane both at 11.6 feet. The storm surge of greater than 20 feet at the head of Buzzards Bay is the largest value in recorded history for the U.S. Atlantic coast.

CONCLUSIONS

Intense hurricanes in the northeast are rare, occurring on average about every 80 years. We know from history, however, that this interval may be as short as 16 years between storms, or as long as 180 years. Of particular concern to residents and emergency management officials are the areas at the heads of Buzzards and Narragansett Bays. These vulnerable areas should expect to face very high storm tides sometime in the future. The question is not if, but when. Emergency management agencies at all levels should redouble their efforts to have viable evacuation plans in these locations as well as educational programs at all age levels to highlight this potentially catastrophic problem. Many generations may come and go before the next intense hurricane hits, but the potential will always be there.

Table 6.1

Month Day	Year	Landfall Location	Pressure (mb)	SLOSH Over Water 1-minute Wind (mph)	Radius of Maximum Winds RMW (mi.)	Translational Direction And Speed (mph)	Storm Tide Providence (ft.)	Storm Tide Head of Buzzards Bay (ft.)
8/26	1635	Long Island	938	132	35	NE/40	14.0*	>20.0*
		Connecticut	939	130	35	NE/40		
9/23	1815	Long Island	956	122	30	NNE/47	14.4	15.9
		Connecticut	957	122	30	NNE/47		
9/21	1938	Long Island	941	132	30	N/40	15.8	14.1
		Connecticut	946	129	30	N/38		
8/31	1954	Long Island	955	130	25	NNE/47	14.8	13.4
	(Carol)	Connecticut	957	127	25	NNE/47		

*Denotes storm surge

SECTION 7

THE SEA ISLAND HURRICANE OF 1893

The storm tide from this hurricane caused the deaths of several thousand people in the Sea Islands of South Carolina. Since the settlement of the islands no major hurricane had previously caused any flood problems and the inhabitants were unaware of the risks. Many people were living and farming at low elevations. The hurricane occurred at night and undoubtedly caused added confusion and chaos which resulted in many drowning deaths. The storm tide ranged from 12 to 16 feet above sea level and totally inundated several of the islands. Other islands have elevations above 15 feet and on these islands, most of the inhabitants survived. A history of life in the Sea Islands of South Carolina before the hurricane, its impact on the inhabitants during the event and the painful recovery is told in The Great Sea Island Storm of 1893 by the Marschers (2001). This hurricane seems to be one of the largest on the Atlantic coast when measured by the radius of the 1000 millibar contour. It caused extensive wind damage to every county in South Carolina, parts of eastern Georgia and the southern part of North Carolina. It was much larger than hurricane Hugo in 1989 although not as intense at landfall. It was possibly as intense before it made landfall. The center made landfall near Savannah, Georgia and passed between Augusta, Georgia and Columbia, South Carolina as it re-curved up the eastern seaboard.

METEOROLOGICAL DATA

Meteorological observations at the Weather Bureau Offices in Savannah and Charleston were taken during the hurricane. As the center passed over Savannah, the wind speed dropped to 10 miles per hour and a 958 millibar pressure was recorded. The maximum wind speed recorded was 72 miles per hour. At Charleston the maximum wind speed was 96 miles per hour with a gust to 120 miles per hour and a pressure of 985 millibars.

Two steps were taken to determine the track of the hurricane. First, twice daily surface pressure observations from stations in the eastern U. S. were plotted and analyzed to determine preliminary center positions while the hurricane was over land. Second, an extensive literature and newspaper search was conducted in 6 cities in the southeast for additional information. The newspapers included the Savannah Morning News, The News and Courier of Charleston, Columbia's The State, The Augusta Chronicle, the Charlotte Observer and the local newspaper in Lynchburg, Virginia. The newspaper search turned up local stories about wind shifts and occasional references to lulls. Some individuals reported meteorological pressure and wind observations. These all helped to determine not only the track and timing of the center passage, but the central pressure as well. Additional observations came from the Naval Observatory in Washington, D.C. Finally, The 1893 Charleston Yearbook contained both meteorological and hydrographic data that was accumulated by the local Weather Bureau meteorologist on the hurricane's impact at Charleston, South Carolina.

HYDROGRAPHIC DATA

High water marks were determined at five coastal locations and were all measured relative to mean sea level. In South Carolina locations and heights were Charleston at 10.1 feet, Beaufort at

12.6 feet and Bluffton at 13.5 feet. Likewise, in Georgia they were Fort Pulaski at 14 to 15 feet and Isle of Hope at 12.5 feet.

DISCUSSION

Figure 7.1 shows the Weather Bureau stations where twice daily surface pressures were recorded and reduced to sea level. Nassau in the Bahamas is included because it had one pressure observation that helped fix the center of the hurricane on the 26th of August. Figures 7.2 and 7.3 are examples of the observed surface pressures and analysis for August 27 at 8 pm and August 28 at 8 am respectively. The 1000 millibar contour is highlighted in red. The red line is the final track with the 12-hour positions labeled. The swath made by connecting the 1000 millibar contours is shown in Figure 7.4. The reason for this becomes apparent when viewing Figure 7.5. The figure shows the track of the hurricane (the 1000 millibar swath), the counties that reported damage (in red) and the projected additional counties that probably had damage but did not report it (in orange). The damage on the right hand side of the track extends over to the 1000 millibar contour but only about one-half the distance on the left hand side. Every county in the state of South Carolina had damage. The impact of this large hurricane to South Carolina and North Carolina was much greater than that caused by hurricane Hugo in 1989. Figure 7.6 is included to give the reader a feel for hurricane size as measured by the radius of the 1000 millibar contour in nautical miles for hurricane Andrew in 1992 that affected South Florida, hurricane Hugo in 1989 and the 1893 hurricane. Charleston, South Carolina was used as a center point.

The observed wind speeds and pressures at the Savannah and Charleston Weather Bureau offices during the hurricane are plotted in Figures 7.7 and 7.8 respectively. Although Savannah was in the eye of the hurricane, the city was located inland away from the coast and the wind speeds were reduced by frictional drag. The maximum recorded wind speed was only 72 miles per hour before the eye arrived. Since the hurricane was moving about 15 miles per hour at landfall the radius of maximum winds in front of the hurricane was estimated at about 25 statute miles. Charleston recorded a higher wind speed of 96 miles per hour with gusts of up to 120 miles per hour. The City of Charleston is located on the west side of Charleston Harbor with a good wind exposure from the ocean to the east-northeast and east, which was the case when the maximum wind was recorded. This wind speed seems high because the center of the storm was about a hundred miles to the southwest and the central pressure at Savannah was only 958 millibars. The only way to obtain this wind speed is to spread the pressure gradient toward Charleston and lower the central pressure. This was done by creating a larger secondary RMW and creating lower central pressure values before landfall. Figure 7.9 is the track of the hurricane with hourly positions labeled in Local Standard Time along with the central pressure values in millibars. As the hurricane made landfall at about 11 pm with a central pressure of 940 millibars, it began to fill quickly-so that it was 957 millibars near Savannah. Filling continued but at a decreasing rate as the hurricane slowly accelerated to the north.

The two circles represent the maximum winds at the specified RMWs. The first one is 25 statute miles as determined from the Savannah observations and the second is 60 statute miles and is the one required to produce a wind speed of approximately 95 miles per hour at Charleston. The strong winds at the 60 statute mile RMW do not appear to be reflected in the Savannah wind record. Since the hurricane is moving about 15 miles per hour near landfall one might expect to see a wind speed maximum about 4 hours before the minimum wind speed in the Savannah wind record. This would be about 9 pm LST. Instead the trace shows a minimum. There is a secondary maximum near 10 pm LST and could be a reflection of the secondary RMW ahead of the hurricane.

SLOSH MODEL SIMULATION

A SLOSH model simulation was made with the data shown in Figure 7.9. The RMW used was 60 statute miles. An additional simulation was made with 25 statute miles and comparison with the run made at 60 statute miles was made. The 25 statute mile SLOSH simulation failed to produce much surge at Charleston and Beaufort whereas the 60 statute mile simulation gave good results everywhere. SLOSH model hydrographs and hind cast tide model hydrographs were produced at all five locations shown in Figure 7.10. The two hydrographs were added together to get a storm tide hydrograph. The maximum storm tide value was compared to the measured high water mark at that location. Figures 7.11 through 7.15 show the calculations at the 5 locations and the comparisons. The results are very good at all locations except at Isle of Hope, Georgia where the results seem too low. This particular high water mark was actually the height of a debris line at the base of an oak tree behind a church in Isle of Hope. It is possible that the water was higher at this location and as the storm tide went down the debris settled at the base of the tree. Any debris left higher up on the trunk of the tree would likely have been washed or blown off by the wind or driving rain.

The SLOSH model shows that over the Sea Islands the maximum storm tide elevations ranged from 12 to 16 feet above sea level.

Figure 7.16 is the comparisons of the SLOSH model one-minute over water winds to the observed winds at Charleston. Overall the comparison is good with the SLOSH model maximum wind about 5 miles per hour less than the observed wind speed. No comparison was done for Savannah because only the 60 statute mile RMW was used in the simulation. The maximum wind generated by the SLOSH model at the RMW of 60 statute miles was 100 miles per hour.

SUMMARY FOR THE 1893 SEA ISLAND HURRICANE

This was an extremely large hurricane. Two RMWs were present in the hurricane. One was 25 statute miles and the other was 60 statute miles. Only the 60 statute mile RMW was used for the SLOSH model simulation, which produced good comparisons with the observed data except at the Isle of Hope. The maximum observed wind speed at Charleston was 95 miles per hour with a minimum pressure of 985 millibars. At Savannah the maximum wind was 72 miles per hour with a minimum pressure of 958 millibars. The maximum wind calculated by the SLOSH model was 100 miles per hour. It was estimated that the hurricane had a pressure near landfall of 940 millibars and rapidly filled to 957 millibars near Savannah. Observed and calculated winds suggest a category 2 hurricane at landfall.

The storm tide generated by the SLOSH model ranged from 12 to 16 feet above sea level in the Sea Islands and was supported by observations. These water elevations resulted in several thousand casualties.

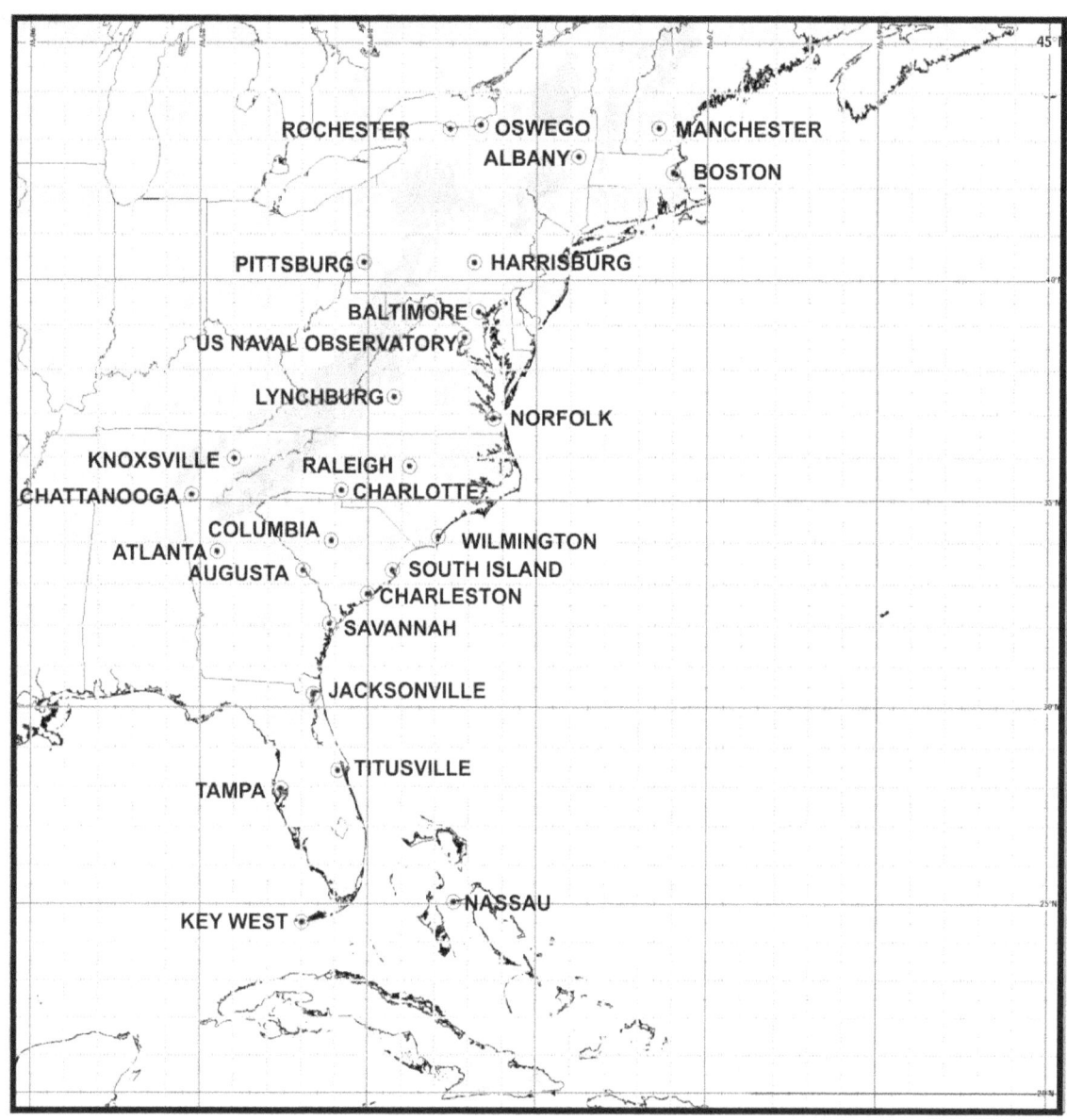

Figure 7.1 Weather Bureau locations used in the study of the 1893 hurricane.

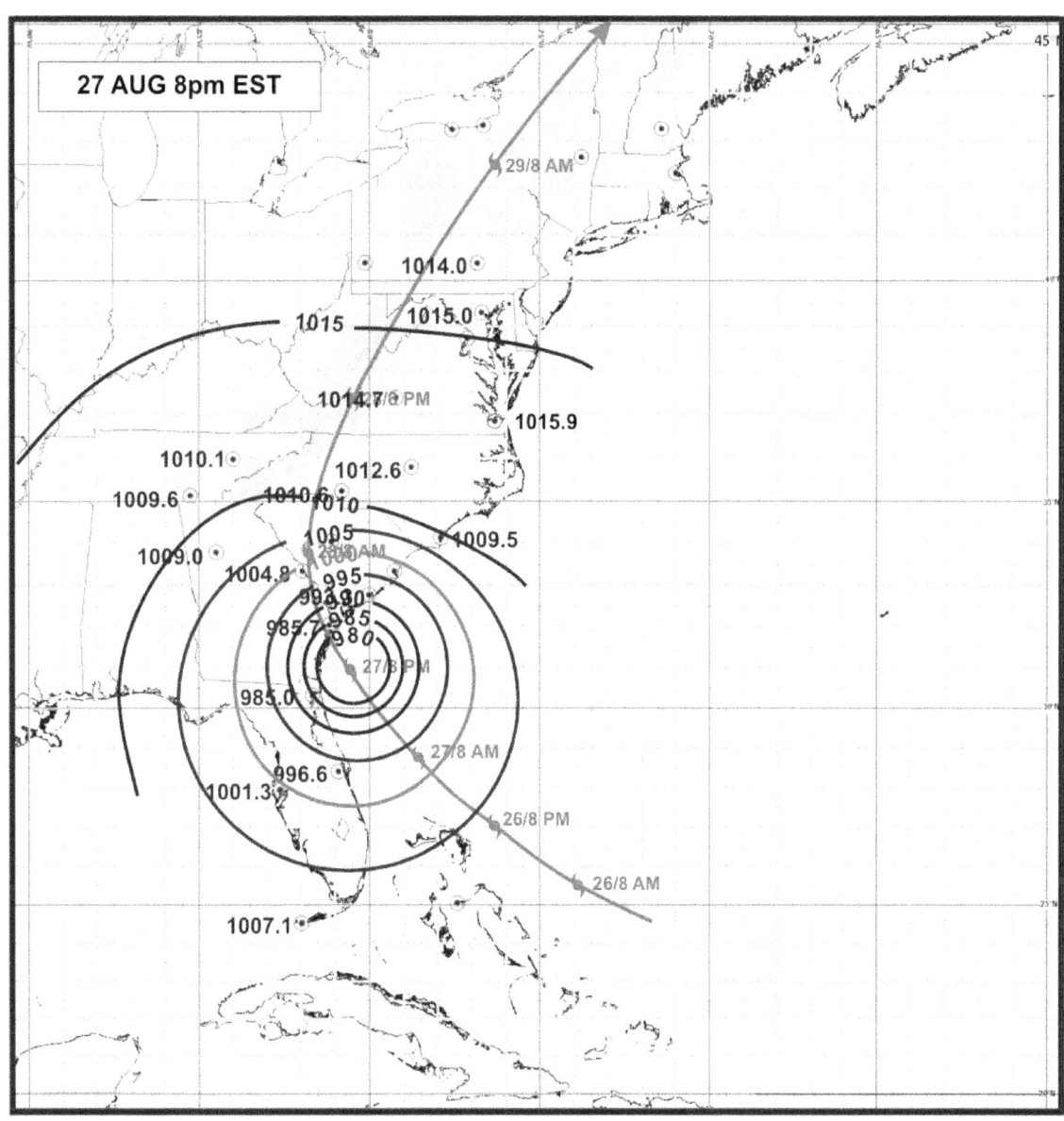

Figure 7.2 Observed pressures and analyzed field for the 1893 hurricane. The track of the hurricane is shown with 12-hour locations labeled with day and Local Standard Time.

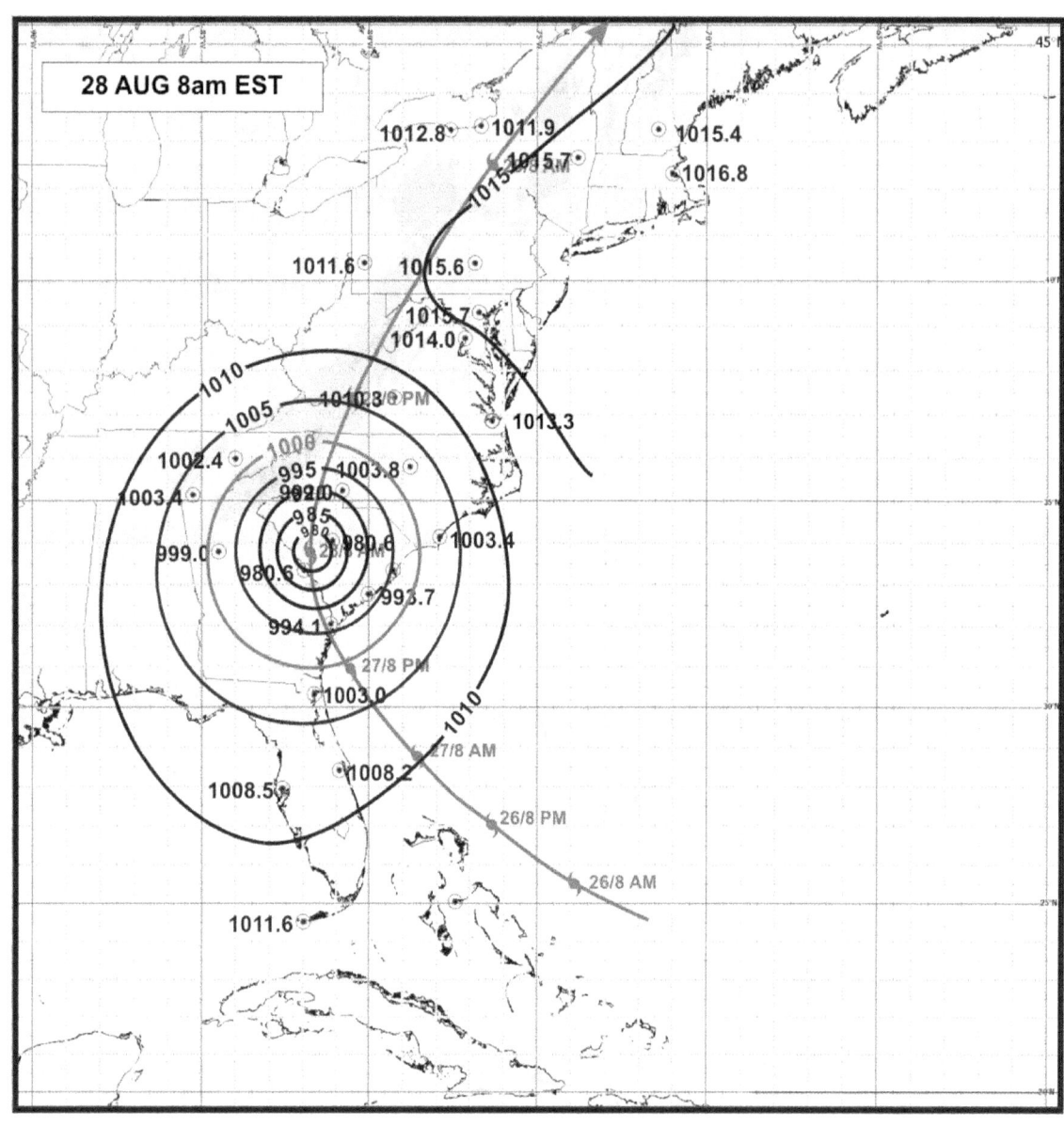

Figure 7.3 Same as Figure 7.2 except 12 hours later. At this time the center was located between Augusta, Georgia and Columbia, South Carolina. Both locations were reporting 980.6 millibar.

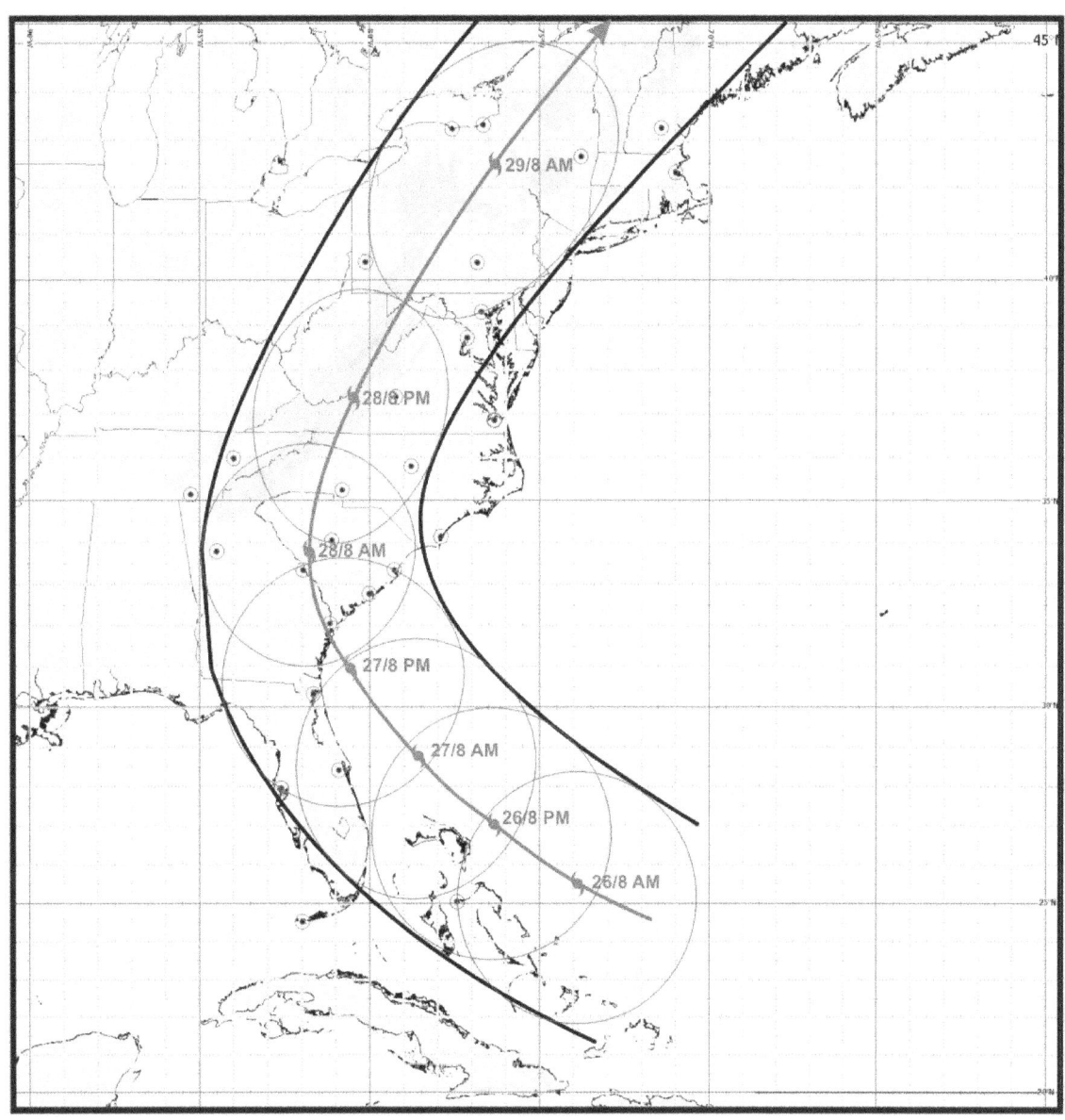

Figure 7.4 Track of the 1893 hurricane and the swath of the 1000 millibar contour.

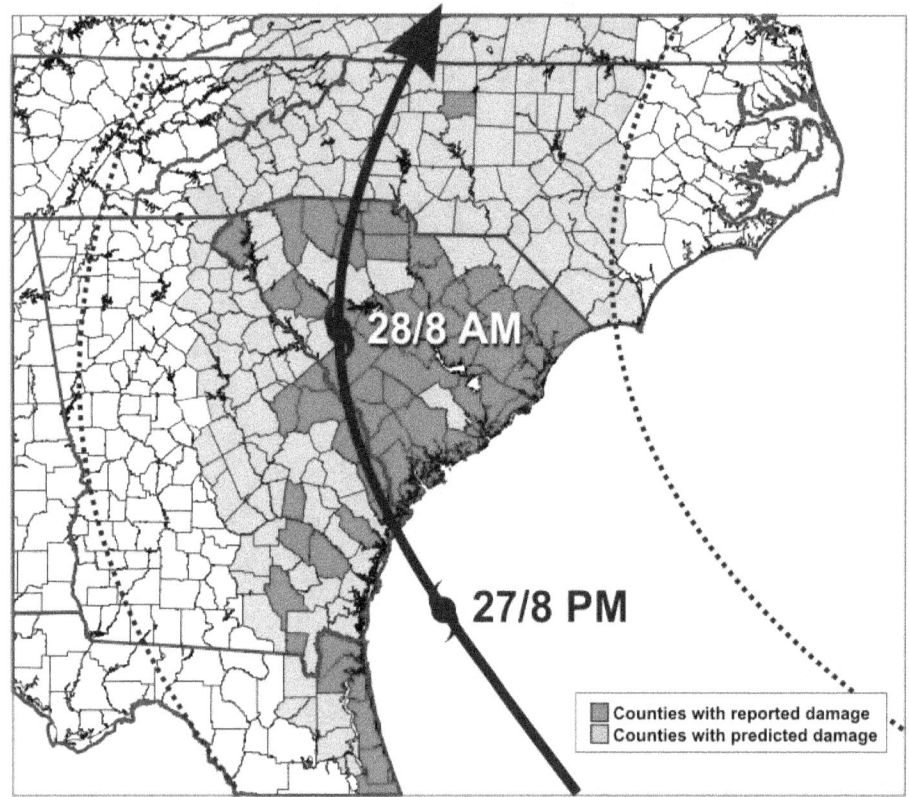

Figure 7.5 Reported and predicted damage in the 1893 hurricane. Dotted lines represent the swath of the 1000 millibar contour. Track shown with 12-hour positions labeled with day and Local Standard Time.

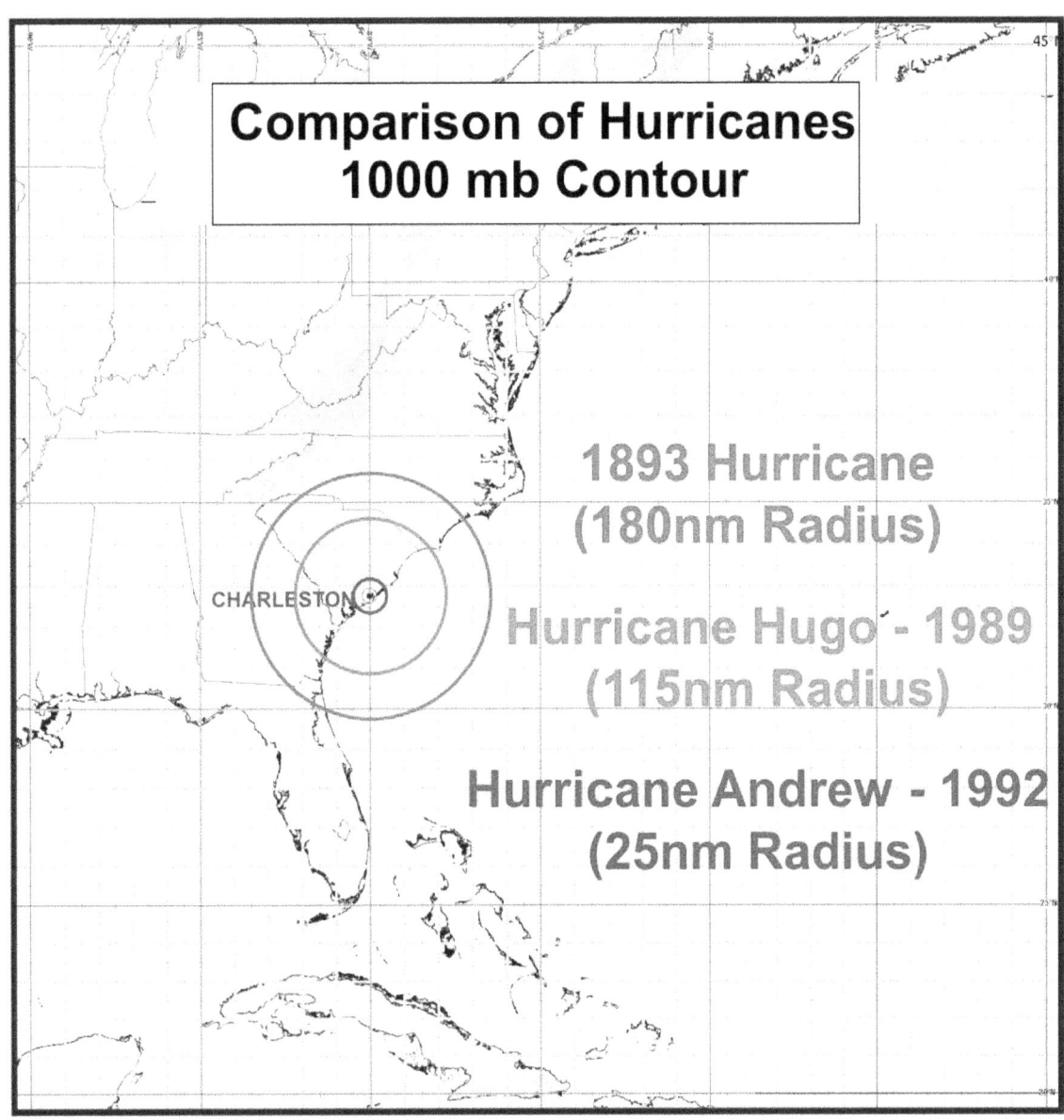

Figure 7.6 Comparison of the size of the 1000 millibar contour in the 1893 hurricane to two other intense hurricanes.

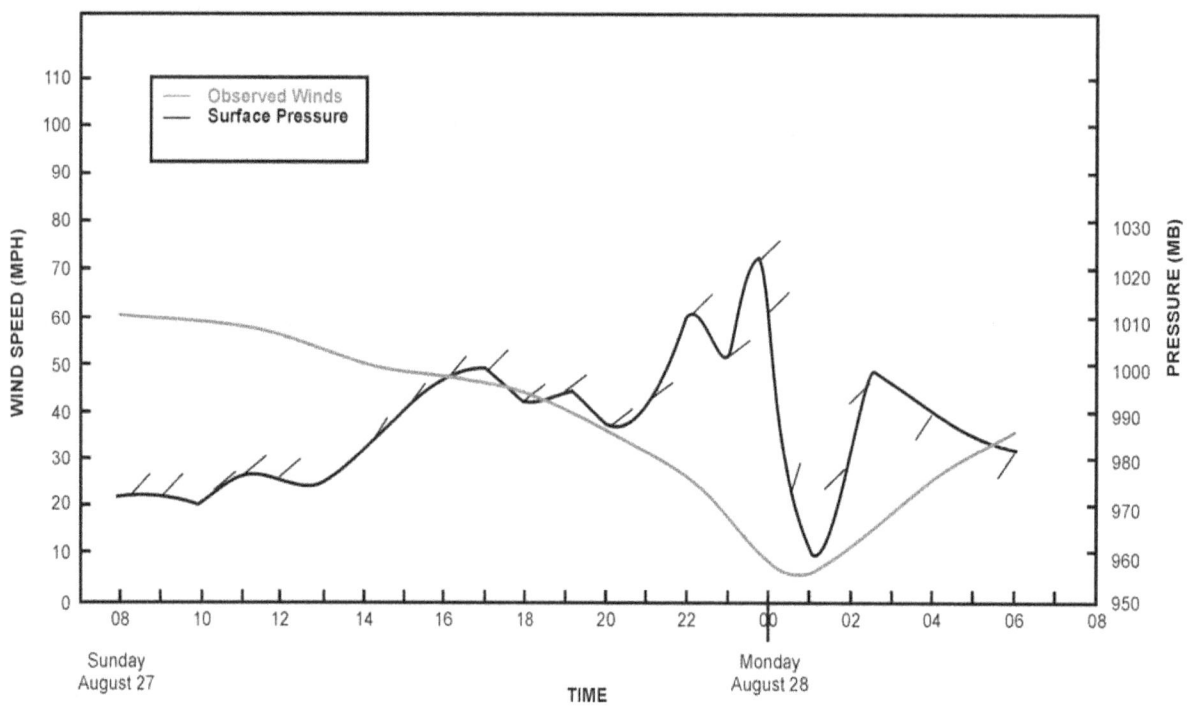

Figure 7.7 Plot of observed wind speed and direction and pressure for the 1893 hurricane at Savannah, Georgia.

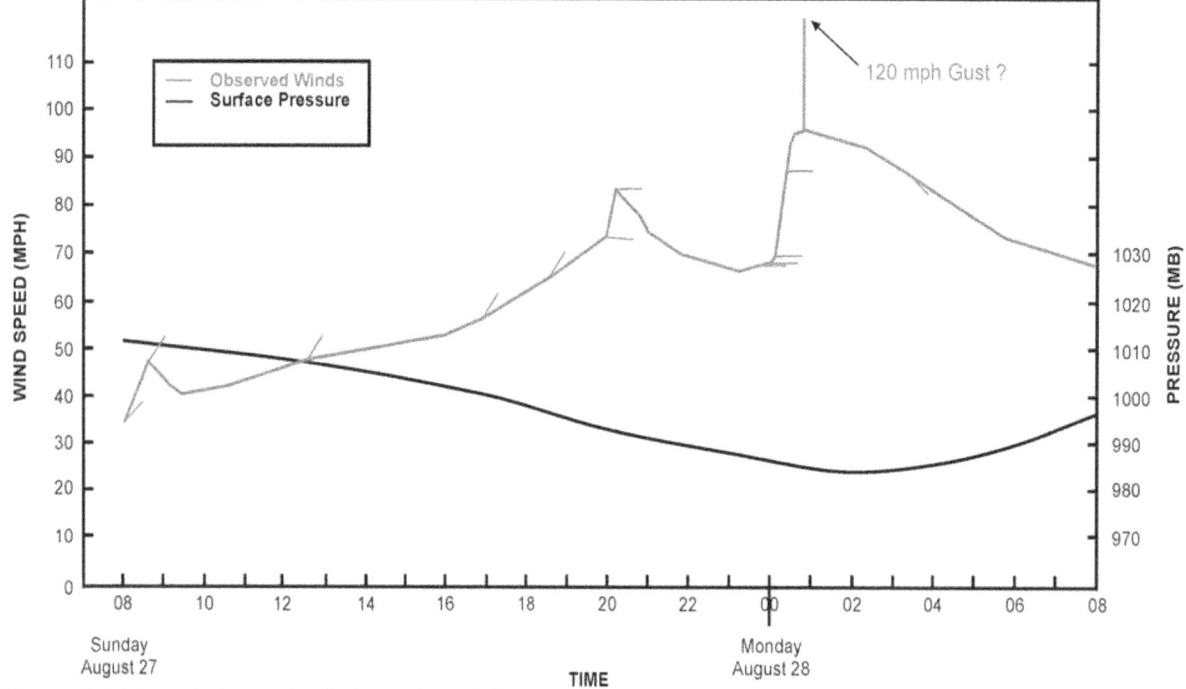

Figure 7.8 Plot of observed wind speed and direction and pressure for the 1893 hurricane at Charleston, South Carolina.

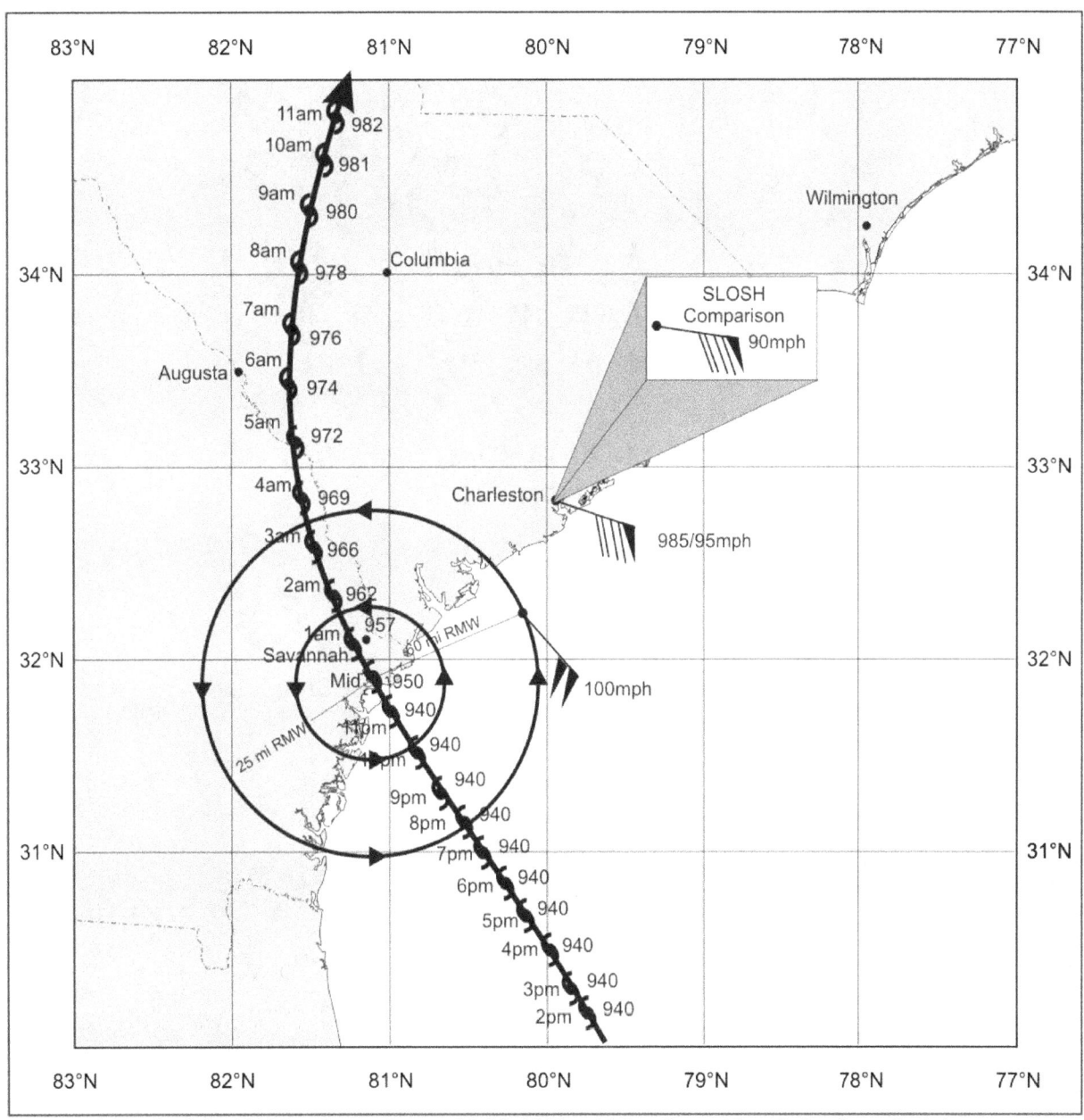

Figure 7.9 Track of the 1893 hurricane, August 27-28, 1893, with hourly positions in local standard time, pressure in millibars and SLOSH model maximum over water 1-minute wind speed in miles per hour. Circles represent location of maximum wind with radius given in statute miles. Wind vectors show where maximum wind is occurring at that time. Wind barbs in mph. At Charleston, the observed wind vector is compared to SLOSH.

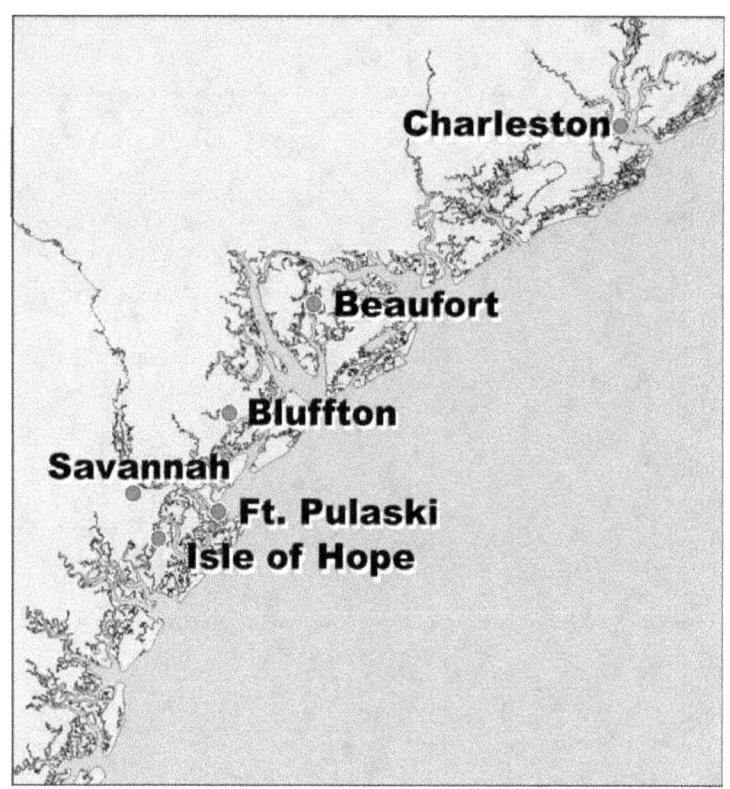

Figure 7.10 Locations where the observed high water marks were compared to the SLOSH/TIDE model value. Savannah is shown for reference only.

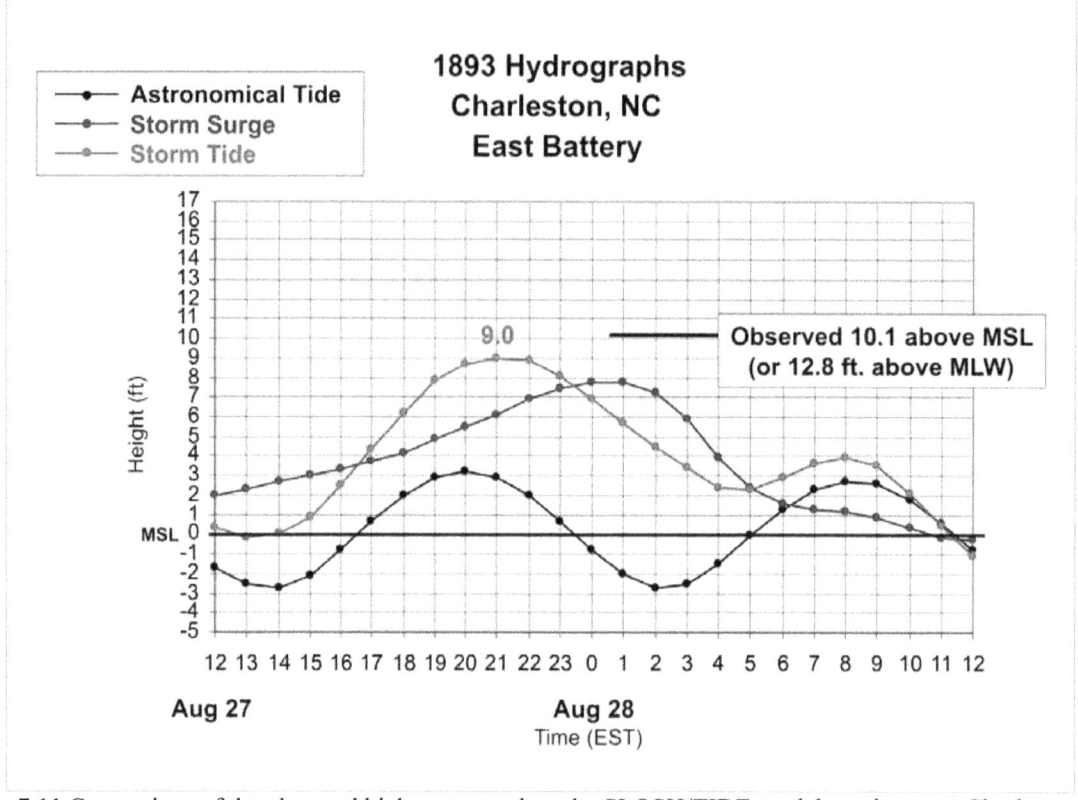

Figure 7.11 Comparison of the observed high water mark to the SLOSH/TIDE model maximum at Charleston.

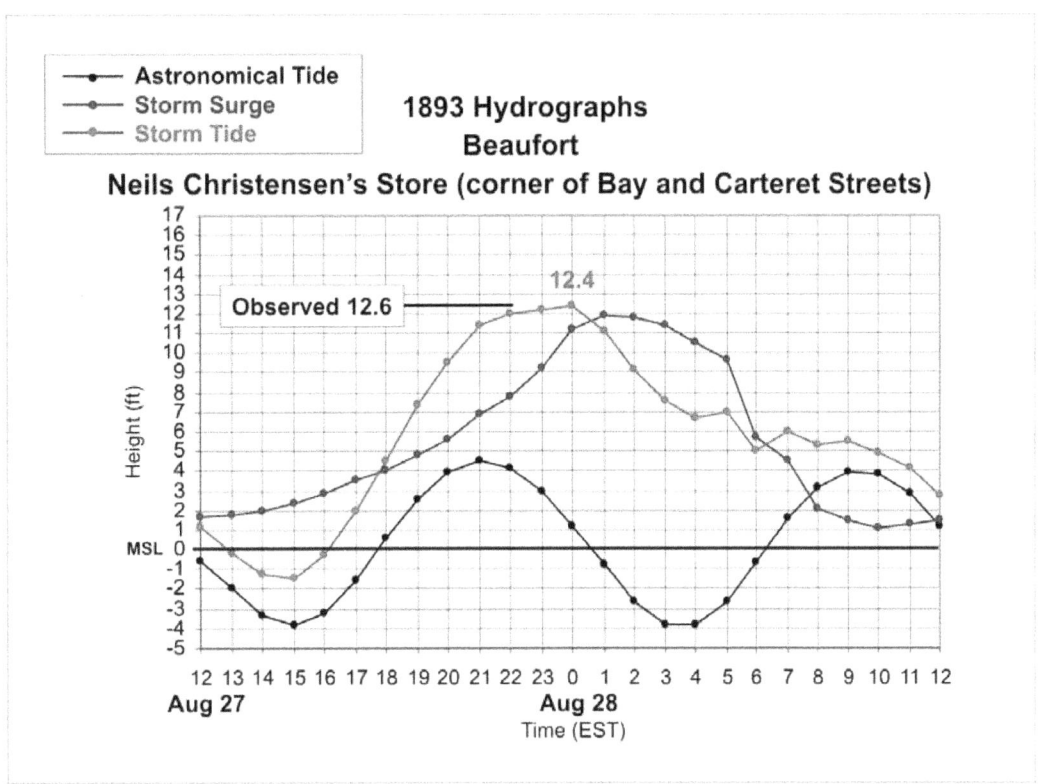

Figure 7.12 Comparison of the observed high water mark to the SLOSH/TIDE model maximum at Beaufort.

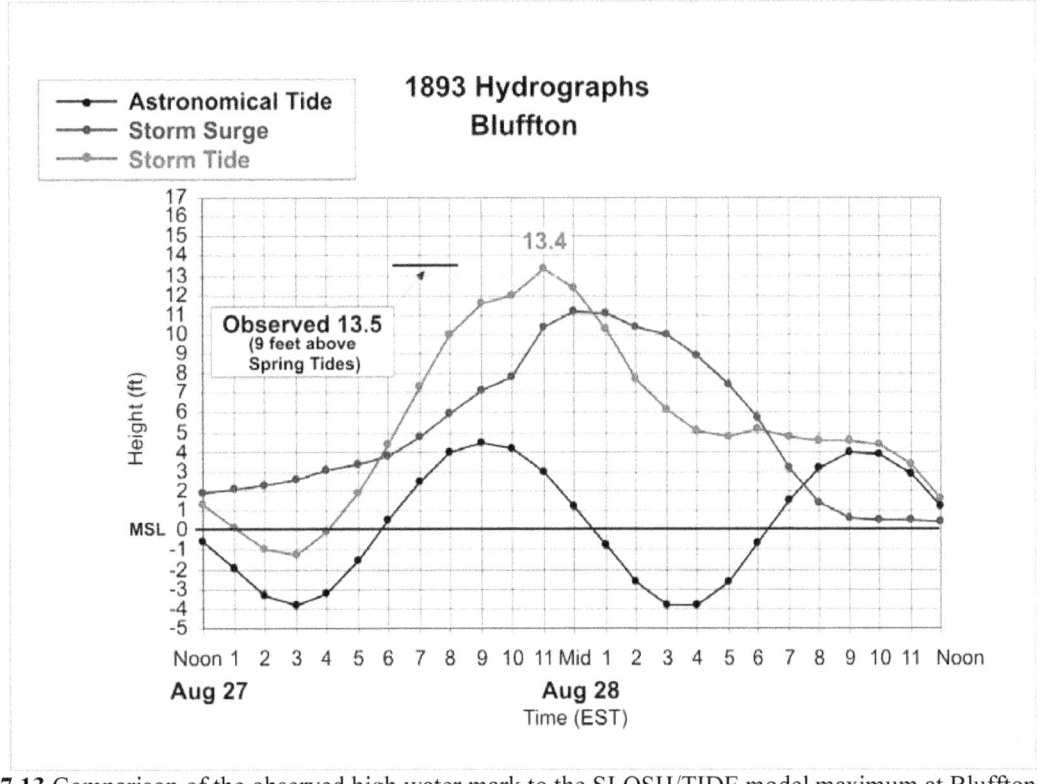

Figure 7.13 Comparison of the observed high water mark to the SLOSH/TIDE model maximum at Bluffton.

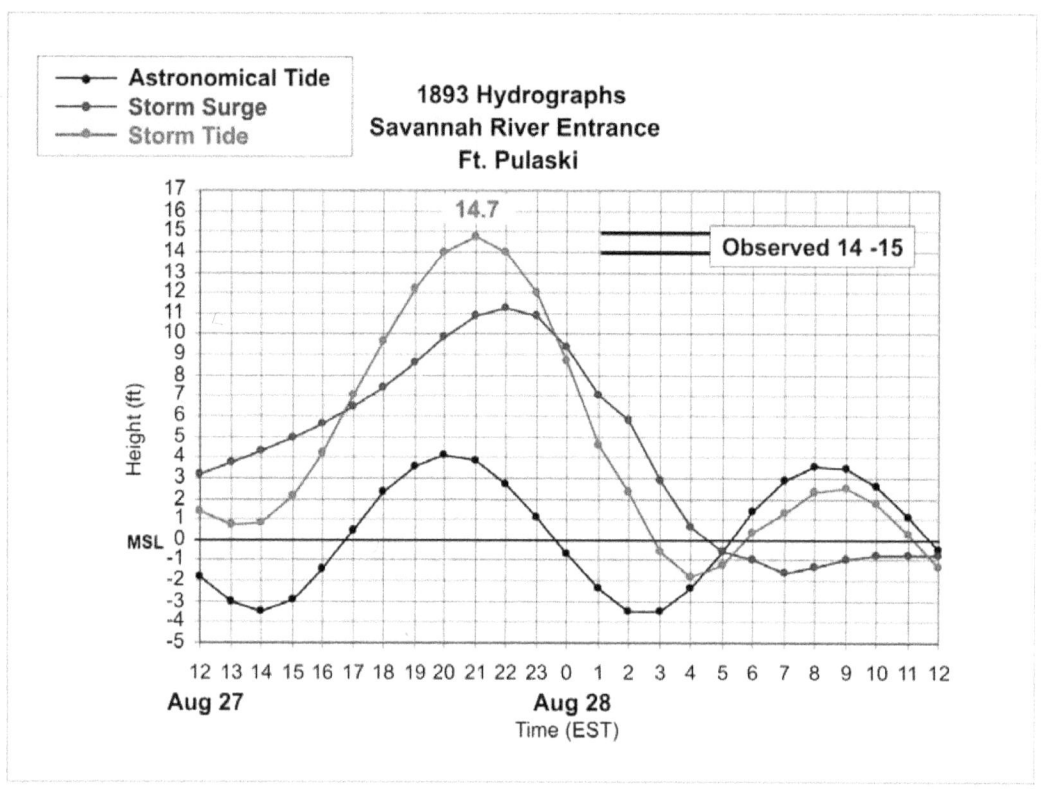

Figure 7.14 Comparison of the observed high water mark to the SLOSH/TIDE model maximum at Ft. Pulaski.

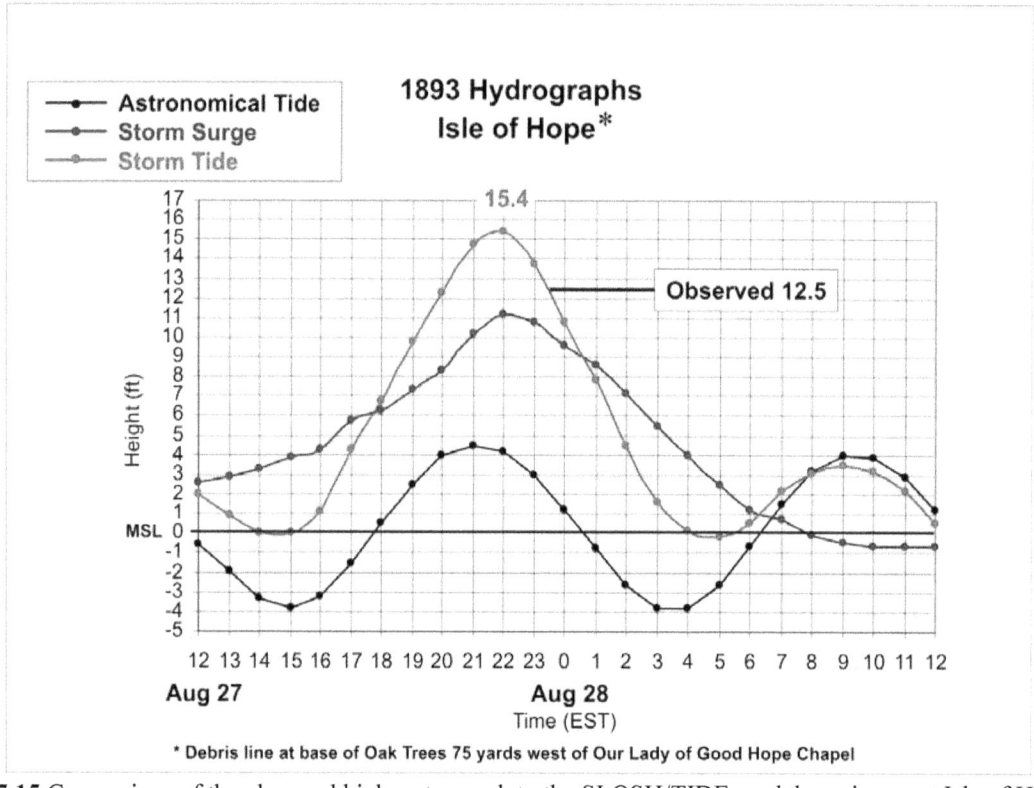

Figure 7.15 Comparison of the observed high water mark to the SLOSH/TIDE model maximum at Isle of Hope.

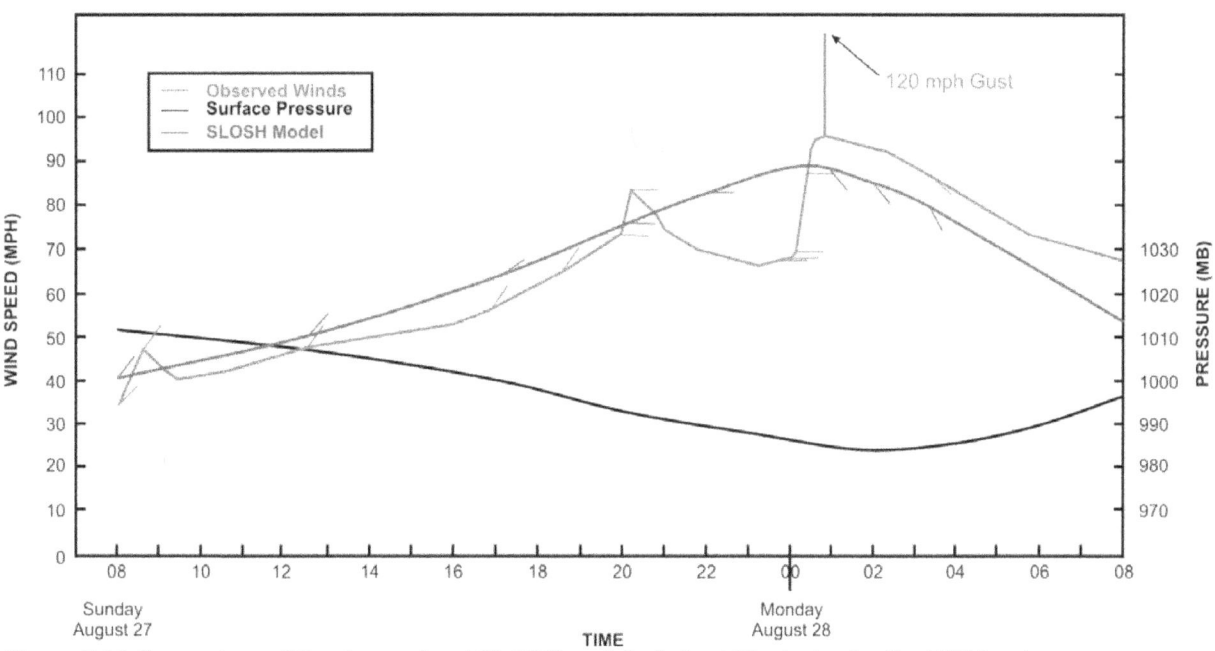

Figure 7.16 Comparison of the observed and SLOSH model winds at Charleston for the 1893 hurricane.

SECTION 8

THE 1935 LABOR DAY HURRICANE

The Labor Day Hurricane of 1935 was the most intense ever hit the U. S. mainland in recorded history. Its central pressure at landfall on Craig Key in the Florida Keys was observed at 892 millibars. The barometer that recorded this value was borrowed from its owner by the Meteorologist in Charge of the Miami Weather Bureau Office and sent to the Bureau of Standards where it was tested in a pressure chamber. The test proved that the barometer was accurate, something which had been questioned due to the low reading during the storm. Several miles to the northeast a value of 899 millibars was observed and several miles to the southwest a value of 917 millibars was observed. Several estimates of the maximum wind speeds have been made over the years. This section will produce a SLOSH model maximum wind for this hurricane to add to the estimates.

The hurricane produced a storm tide that piled up against the Flagler railroad embankments that ran the length of each island. On the right side of the eye, the water was driven from the southeast. When it was high enough to over-top the embankment, it flowed down the other side like a waterfall into Florida Bay. On the left hand side of the eye the water was driven from the north and when it was high enough to over-top the embankment it flowed down the other side, in a similar fashion, into the Atlantic Ocean.

The hurricane killed about 400 people. Most of these were on the right side of the eye. Residents faced a combination of incredible wind speeds, air filled with flying debris, sand, shells, stinging rain and salt spray. These things, along with the flow of water caused many victims to be blown and/or washed out into Florida Bay.

A train sent from Miami to evacuate the veteran camps was delayed and arrived at Islamorada just before the worst of the hurricane occurred. All of the coach cars on the train along with several freight cars on a side track were moved off the tracks by a combination of wind and water. Most people who took refuge in these cars survived. The locomotive was too heavy to be blown or washed off the tracks, but water rose into the cab and people scrambled to survive this rising water.

Breaking waves added significant water elevations on top of the storm tide. Based upon data from other historical hurricanes in the Florida Keys, this contribution could be as large as the storm tide itself.

METEOROLOGICAL DATA

The Monthly Weather Review article by McDonald (1935) is the main source of information for this hurricane. Post hurricane interviews with survivors were a second source. Surface pressure data at stations in the Southeast was obtained for several days before and after landfall in the Keys. The data was available twice daily at 8 am and 8 pm Local Standard Time. Analysis of this data allowed a track to be generated that was modified by additional observations.

The following eyewitness accounts come from the U.S. Army Corps Report (1956):

1. Statement of E. B. Parker, F.E.R.A. Employee No. 59, Upper Matecumbe Key
   Mr. Parker stated that his house was located about 300 feet south of the Matecumbe Hotel, and that it was destroyed except for one small corner in which he and his 10 children took refuge and survived the storm. He stated the water rose suddenly and receded with equal swiftness and was at its peak for about 45 minutes; the wind again blew from the northeast and was at its peak from that direction at about 6:45 pm, September 2; it shifted to east about 8:45 pm. The barometer fell rapidly from 3:30 pm to 5:30 pm and the lowest reading he observed- which he had his son check- was 26.55 inches at 9:30 pm.

2. Statement of L. Russel, Islamorada
   Mr. Russel lived on Windley Key; he left the key about 7 pm, September 2, on the train sent to evacuate the veteran's camp. The wind at the key was from the northeast when he left and until he reached the Islamorada Station; at that point the wind gradually shifted to the southeast and the water rose with the wind. All windows on the east side of the train were broken which indicates the direction of the wind. The water rose rapidly- but not with a rush- and descended rapidly. Water was 2 feet deep in the train coaches before they left the tracks at Islamorada Station about 9:30 pm and it rose as high as Mr. Russel's chest after the train was derailed; there was no lull in the wind.

3. Statement of Bob Combs, Chief Deputy Sheriff, Tavernier
   Mr. Combs stated that the water rose 3-1/2 to 4 feet above the highway 50 feet south of the Tavernier Post Office. He stated that on October 3 he visited Alligator reef Lighthouse and Mr. Duncan, the lightkeeper, showed him where panes of glass in the structure surrounding the light were broken out by wind and wave action 136 feet above high water; one glass on the southeast side was the only one not broken. Mr. Duncan also showed Mr. Combs where steel doors- which opened outward- in the keeper's quarters, about 50 feet above the water, were pushed inward through the doorstops; interior wooden doors were broken and ripped off the hinges. Mr. Duncan estimated the wind at 175-200 miles per hour.

4. Statement of C. Marvin Thompson, Islamorada
   Mr. Thompson stated that after his house was destroyed he went to the Florida East Coast Railway freight station and when that began to break up about 8 pm he left the station with his 2 brothers and 11 others, among whom was Mr. Sheldon, superintendent of the veteran's camp. They took refuge in one of two freight cars on the siding of the Islamorada station. The car in which the men took refuge contained about 40 drums of oil and the other car, which was coupled to the one they were in, contained 50 tons of cement. Since he was shut in the freight car, Mr. Thompson could only estimate wind directions. When he entered the car at 8 pm no water was standing on the ground; after being in the car about 30 minutes, the water came with a rush that turned the cars over on their sides on the west side of the track; about 10 minutes later a passenger train which had pulled in on the main-line track abreast of the freight cars turned over on top of the freight cars. Before the freight cars capsized, water was 10 inches deep over the car floors, having risen to that height from ground level in about 30 minutes. After the car turned on its side, Mr. Thompson stood on a gasoline drum and the water rose until it reached a point above his waist (or about 6 feet above ground level at that point). The sidetrack on which the freight cars stood was not washed out and is still in place; the

adjoining main-line track on which the passenger train stood was washed out. The lull of the storm came 3 to 4 hours after the freight cars turned over, or about midnight. The lull lasted about 35 minutes and the wind then shifted to the southwest. Water fell as rapidly as it rose. About 3:30 am the following morning the men chopped their way out of the freight car with tools that had been passed into them.

5. Statement of R. L. Bow, State Road Department, Lower Matecumbe Key
   Mr. Bow is in charge of much of the State Road Department's road and bridge operations in the Keys; he went through the storm aboard the U.S. dredge *Sarasota,* anchored in a creek at Lower Matecumbe Key near the ferry slip. He stated that the wind began in the north and ended in the south; water came with a rush after the lull, when the wind shifted to the south; water fell gradually. The lull lasted 55 minutes- from 8:45 to 9:40 pm, September 2- and water reached a height estimated from water marks left on the railroad at 18 to 20 feet above mean low tide. The lowest graduation on Mr. Bow's barometer was 27.80, but the needle fell below that mark at 8:45 pm to what he and others aboard the dredge estimated as 27.55. Concerning the height of water at Windley Key, Mr. Bow states that the highest water mark they have checked by level is 15-1/2 feet above the State Road Department's plane of mean low water.

6. Report of J. E. Duane, Long Key
   Passage of the hurricane is graphically described in a report submitted by J. E. Duane, cooperative observer for the Weather Bureau and manager of a fish camp on Long Key, over which the center passed. Extracts from his report follow, in the chronological order of his observations:

   September 2
   2 p.m.- Barometer falling; heavy sea swell and a high tide; heavy rain squalls continued. Wind from N. or NNE., force 6.

   3 p.m.- Ocean swells had changed; the change noted was that large waves were rolling in from the SE., somewhat against winds which were still in N. or NE.

   4 p.m.- Wind still N., increasing to force 9. Barometer dropping 0.01 inches every 5 minutes. Rain continued.

   5 p.m.- Wind N., hurricane force. Swells from the SE.
   6 p.m.- Barometer 28.04; still falling. Heavy rains. Wind still N., hurricane force and increasing. Water rising on the north side of island.

   6:45 p.m.- Barometer 27.90. Wind backing to NW., increasing; plenty of flying timbers, and heavy timber, too. It made no difference as to weight and size. A beam 6 by 8 inches, about 18 feet long, was blown from north side of camp, about 300 yards, through observer's house, wrecking it and nearly striking 3 persons. Water 3 feet from top of railroad grade, or about 16 feet.

   7 p.m.- We were now located in main lodge building of camp; flying timbers had begun to wreck this lodge, and it was shaking on every blast. Water had now reached level of railway on north side of camp. (Editor's note: This was water rapidly piled up from the shallow expanse of Florida Bay, under the drive of northerly hurricane winds.)

9 p.m.- No signs of storm letting up. Barometer still falling very fast.

9:20 p.m.- Barometer 27.22 inches; wind abated. We now heard other noises than the wind and knew the center of storm was over us. We now head for the last and only cottage that I think can or will stand in the blow due to arrive shortly. All hands, 20 in number, gather in this cottage. During this lull, the sky is clear to northward, stars shining brightly and a very light breeze continued; no flat calm. About the middle of the lull which lasted a timed 55 minutes, the sea began to lift up, it seemed, and rise very fast; this from ocean side of camp. I put my flashlight out to sea and could see walls of water which seemed many feet high. I had to race fast to regain entrance of cottage, but water caught me waist deep, although I was only about 60 feet from the doorway of the cottage. Water lifted cottage from its foundations, and it floated.

10:10 p.m.- Barometer now 27.01 inches; wind beginning to blow from SSW.

10:15 p.m.- The first blast from the SSW., full force. House now breaking up; wind seemed stronger than at any time during storm. I glanced at barometer which read 26.98 inches, dropped it in water and was blown outside into sea; got hung up in broken fronds of coconut tree and hung on for dear life. I was then struck by some object and knocked unconscious.

September 3:

2:25 a.m.- I became conscious in tree and found I was lodged about 20 feet above ground. All water had disappeared from island; the cottage had been blown back on the island, from whence the sea receded and left it with all the people safe. Hurricane winds continued until 5 a.m. and during this period terrific lightning flashes were seen. After 5 a.m. strong gales continued throughout day with very heavy rain.

HYDROLOGIC DATA

The U. S. Army Corps of Engineers conducted a post hurricane high water mark survey. Their results were published in the report mentioned above. Many of the marks were debris lines on the railroad embankment. Some of the high water estimates were determined from the accounts mentioned above. Many of the marks were seaweed and sea grass that was lodged in nooks and crannies in the concrete embankments near the bridges.

DISCUSSION

The track of the hurricane was determined from the surface pressure analysis and the fact that it made landfall in the Keys around 9 pm on September 2, and was located near Long Island in the Bahamas on August 31. Figure 8.1 shows the track of the hurricane. Six-hourly positions are labeled with time, date and central pressure in millibars. All of the pressure values are estimated except the value near the Keys. The system was very likely a depression as it passed over Long Island in the Bahamas. The next day it was probably a strong tropical storm and became a hurricane early in the morning on September 2. (Author's note: The deepening rates before landfall might have been similar to hurricane Wilma's in 2005 when it was located in the Yucatan Channel.) After landfall it probably began a weakening trend that continued until it made a second landfall on the Gulf coast of northern Florida. Figure 8.1 also shows the minimum pressure observed at several locations in Florida. The hurricane was moving between 9 to 10 miles per hour at its initial landfall in the Keys.

Figure 8.2 is the track of the hurricane with hourly positions showing the time and pressure. Also shown is a circle representing the location of the maximum winds. The radius of 6 statute miles was mostly determined by information from the survivor's accounts.

The U.S. Army Corps of Engineers produced a high water mark profile from Long Key to southern Key Largo. The values range from18 feet near the RMW on the right side to about 10 feet at the southern end of Key Largo. The high water mark profile figure also contains a poor quality profile of the height of the Flagler railroad. Thus, the height of the water above the railroad can be approximated. The railroad embankment acted as a dam for the storm tide and breaking waves until it was over-topped. The author of the report stated that it was estimated that the storm tide near the maximum water elevation of 18 feet was 12 feet and the remaining height was due to wave effects or 6 feet.

SLOSH MODEL SIMULATION

It was hoped that before the completion of this project that the actual as-built survey containing the height of the Flagler railroad could be obtained from the Flagler Museum in Palm Beach, Florida and a SLOSH model grid created with these values, similar to what was done for the 1900 Galveston hurricane in Section 12. This was not possible, so the simulation was done using the current basin configuration. This configuration has barrier elevations that largely reflect the height of U.S. Highway 1. These elevations are generally much lower than the railroad grade present in 1935. Over-topping of U. S. 1 will occur at lower storm tide elevations than if the railroad grade elevations were present. In addition, many of the openings between islands that exist today were closed when the railroad was built, thus creating a greater damming effect in 1935.

A SLOSH model simulation was made with the values shown in figures 8 .1 and 8.2. A small amplitude high tide was occurring in 1935 and was 0.2 feet above mean sea level. This was the initial value used for the SLOSH run.

Even with the current configuration, the results are impressive. Figure 8.3 shows a SLOSH wind speed trace and hydrograph for a point near the RMW on the right hand side of the eye on the ocean side of the Keys. This point would be near the northern end of Lower Matecumbe Key. The SLOSH model one-minute over the water wind speed increases rapidly to 185 miles per hour. Just before the maximum winds arrive, the water rises up from approximately 2 feet at 8 pm to 8 feet at 9 pm. This equates to a rise of about one foot every ten minutes. However, at this location the barrier in the current configuration is only 6 feet and water begins to flow into Florida Bay once this height is reached. The surge continues to rise to a little over 8 feet, and a tremendous amount of water flows over U.S. 1. If the barrier height was raised to 10 feet in the SLOSH model (i.e. configuring a first guess height for the railroad embankment) and the simulation repeated, the water might overtop the new barrier and the final height might be 12 feet.

The description of the wind and the rise of water with time by L. Russel, who was in the train at Islamorada is very similar to what Fig. 8.3 shows. At this location the railroad track elevation was approximately 10 feet above sea level. The U.S. Army Corps profile shows 16 feet at this location (or 6 feet of water above the tracks). This is somewhat verified by Russel because he observes 2 feet of water in the train car before it was pushed over. The floor of the train car was approximately 4 feet above the tracks and the tracks were 10 feet above mean sea level. The added water elevation due to breaking waves at this location appears to be about 4 feet, but it could have been greater.

Mr. Duane's account on the south end of Long Key leaves the reader with some perplexing questions. Before the eye arrives he states that the wind is from the north and that it eventually piles water up to the top of the railroad grade on the north side. The railroad grade according to his description is at 19 feet. The SLOSH model simulation only produces 4 to 5 feet of storm tide at this location. This author believes that this small 4 to 5 feet of surge covered the camp on the north side with about a foot of water above the ground. Large breaking waves rode in on top of the storm tide and piled water against the grade. The wind, blowing at approximately 150 miles per hour, would easily move some of this water over the top of the grade as sheet spray and give the appearance (to someone on the other side of the grade) of over-topping. Mr. Duane was sheltered in a building on the south side of the grade at this time, trying to dodge flying debris. He makes no mention of water on the south side of the grade. In fact, if he had been able to look southward at the ocean, he would have noticed that the strong north winds had pushed water away from the shoreline at that point in time. Shortly thereafter, the eye passed over his location. The strong winds that had been driving the water offshore decreased and the water began to return. It would have looked like a tidal bore as it approached the land and most likely have been several feet high. This is what he described as seeing with his flashlight. The bore rolled in very quickly and caught him before he could get back into the building. (Author's note: The winds were still light at this time.) He does manage to get back into the building and take one last look at the barometer before the winds arrive from the south-southwest. Almost immediately the cottage began to break up and he is blown outside into the water. These winds created a similar scenario on the south side as had previously occurred earlier on the north side. Mr. Duane got hung up in some downed coconut trees and fronds. He and the trees were most likely pushed up onto the railroad embankment. When he regained consciousness, he noted that he was 20 feet above the ground. The railroad embankment is at 19 feet. If he had really been lodged in the top of a coconut tree at a 20 foot elevation, he would probably have been seriously injured getting down. In addition, pictures taken in the aftermath of the storm indicate that almost all the trees in his vicinity were blown down by the hurricane.

SUMMARY FOR THE 1935 LABOR DAY HURRICANE

The hurricane made landfall in the Florida Keys with a central pressure of 892 millibars and SLOSH model calculated winds of 185 miles per hour. The storm tide elevations ranged from 10 to 18 feet and it was estimated that the breaking waves contributed a significant amount to the total height.

Unequivocally, this hurricane could be a category 6 on the Saffir-Simpson Scale, if the scale provided for a storm higher than a category 5. The reasoning is that if category 4 wind speeds are 135 to 155 miles per hour, then category 5 wind speeds must be 156 to 180 miles per hour. Category 6 winds would be 181 to 205 miles per hour. Category 7 would be greater than 205 miles per hour. Based on central pressure, there is roughly a 20 millibar difference between categories. Generally, 900 to 920 millibars is category 5 while 880 to 899 millibars would be category 6. Below 880 millibars would be category 7. Although rare, these "off the scale" hurricanes will occur again.

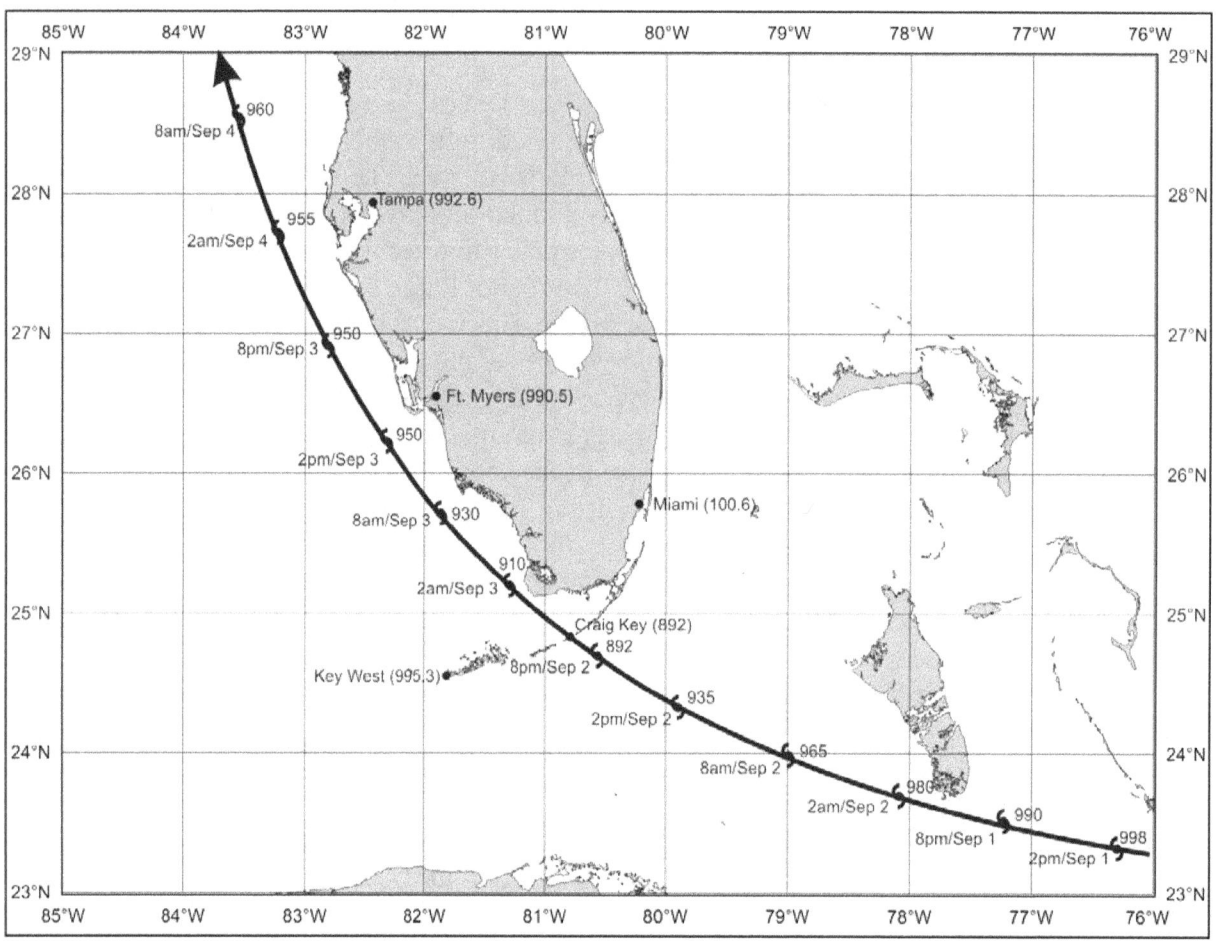

Figure 8.1 Track of the 1935 Labor Day hurricane, September 2-3, 1935. Six-hourly positions are labeled with date and local standard time and pressure in millibars. Values at labeled cities are recorded minimum pressure.

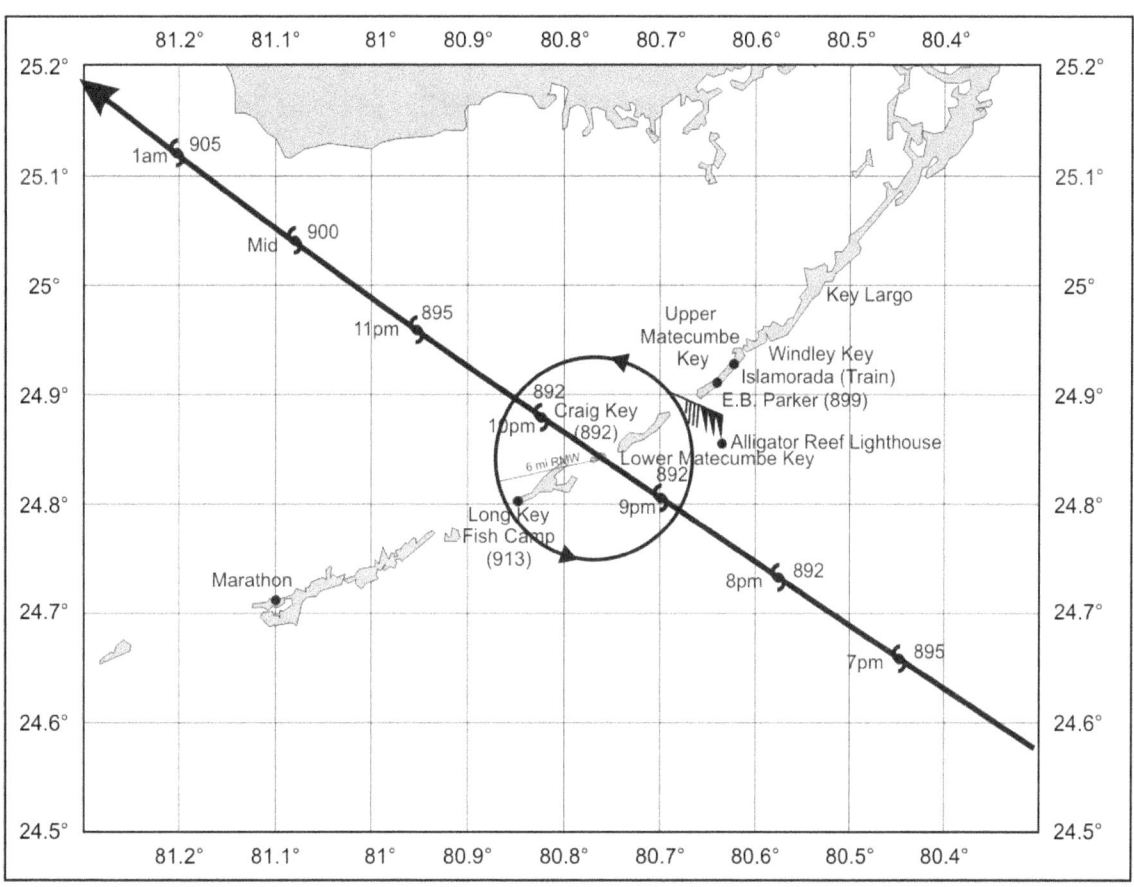

Figure 8.2 Track of the 1935 Labor Day hurricane, September 2-3, 1935. Hourly positions are labeled with local standard time and pressure in millibars. Circle represents location of maximum winds. Maximum wind vector of 180 miles per hour located 6 statute miles from the hurricane center when it is at Craig Key. Wind barbs in mph.

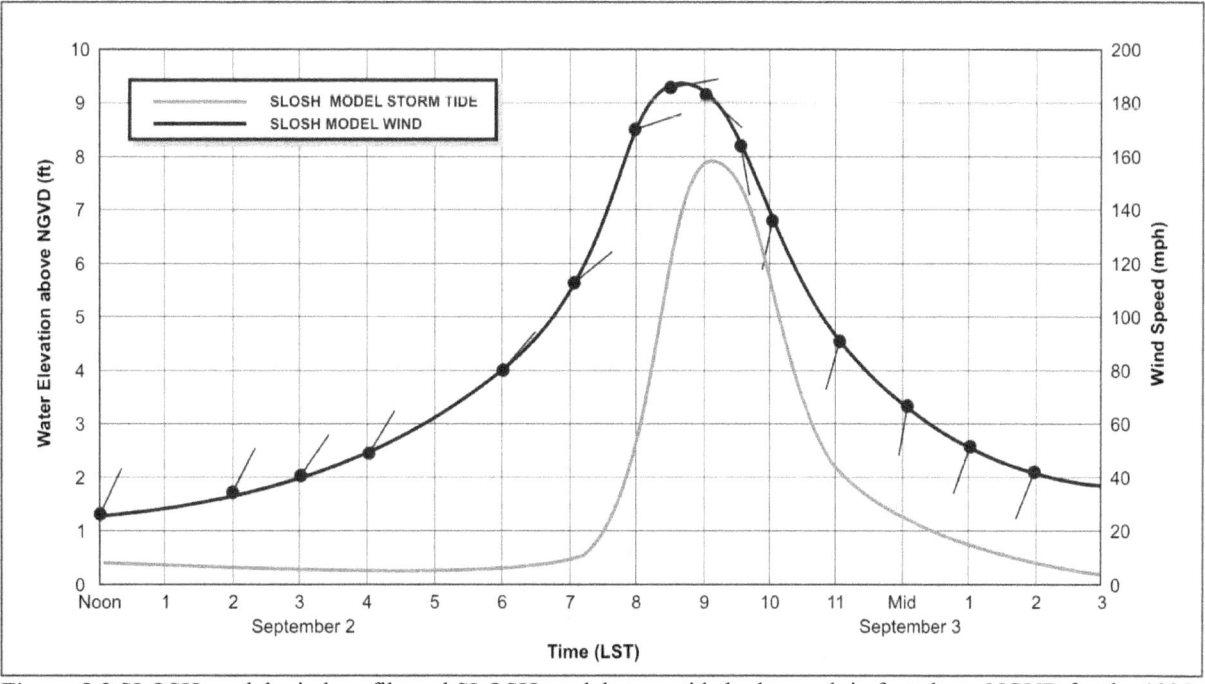

Figure 8.3 SLOSH model wind profile and SLOSH model storm tide hydrograph in feet above NGVD for the 1935 Labor Day hurricane near the RMW on the right side.

–55–

SECTION 9

COMPARISON OF OBSERVED AND SLOSH MODEL STORM TIDE IN TROPICAL STORM ISIDORE (2002)

Isidore was a large tropical storm when it made landfall in southeast Louisiana. Significant storm surge elevations were generated along the southeast Louisiana, Mississippi and Alabama coastlines. Also, Lake Pontchartrain saw a significant rise in water well before tropical storm force winds arrived. As Isidore approached from the south the winds north of the center drove the lake waters towards the southwest. As the center passed, the winds reversed and drove the lake waters toward the northeast and caused flooding in many populated lake front communities.

METEOROLOGICAL DATA

A summary of the history of Hurricane Isidore is given in a report by Avila (2002). The report states that Isidore was a category 3 hurricane in the Gulf of Mexico but weakened to a tropical storm due to its interaction with the Yucatan Peninsula. At the same time the wind field began to expand and eventually a large part of the Gulf of Mexico was covered by tropical storm force winds. Isidore moved northward and made landfall with winds of 55 knots, a minimum pressure of 984 millibars and a RMW of 70 statute miles just west of Grand Isle, LA at 0600 UTC 26 September.

Hourly surface pressure charts were analyzed to track the pressure center from near landfall at 0600 UTC to 1800 UTC when the storm was located in south central Mississippi. Figure 9.1 shows the surface pressure analysis for 1300 UTC on September 26. The pressure center was located just to the northeast of Lake Pontchartrain and the central pressure was estimated at 985 millibars. This was just one millibar higher than 7 hours earlier at landfall. In fact, at 1800 UTC the pressure was only 987 millibars. This represents only 3 millibars of filling in 12 hours and is probably a result of the system passing over very warm marsh land after landfall and the fact that the storm was very large and took longer to fill. Figure 9.2 shows the track of the surface pressure center and the track of the radar center fixes. It is a comparison of a very conservative pressure field to a rapidly changing and subjectively determined radar presentation.

HYDROLOGIC DATA

No high water mark survey was conducted after this storm. However, the U. S. Army Corps of Engineers had a series of recording tide gages throughout the region and these combined with several from the U.S. Geological Service and National Ocean Service, allowed for the creation of a coastal high water mark profile which is shown in Figure 9.3.

The initial water elevations along the northern Gulf coast were elevated prior to the arrival of tropical storm force winds. These elevations are termed the pre-storm tide anomalies and are caused by the disruption of the normal circulation into and out of the Gulf of Mexico. Typically, when a hurricane passes through the Yucatan Channel, such as Isidore did, it enhances the flow of water into the Gulf of Mexico. If the hurricane is strong and has a large wind field to the north, the easterly winds north of Cuba will impede the flow of water out of the Gulf of Mexico and result in an increase in the amount of water in the Gulf of Mexico. Plotted near the bottom of Figure 9.5 is the radius of the 1000 millibar contour and the central pressure with time. This bottom plot shows how Isidore's pressure field and associated wind field grew from about 50 to 200 nautical miles over a three day period as the hurricane approached the Yucatan Peninsula. The result was a rise of water in the Gulf of Mexico and is reflected in the hydrograph for Waveland, Mississippi which is shown in Figure 9.4. Here the pre-storm tide anomaly is fluctuating between 2 and 3 feet above the normal predicted astronomical tide (which is labeled astrotide). The astrotide is what should have been occurring but there was elevated water present and it occurred before the beginning of the storm surge at about 0000 UTC on 26 September. In order for the SLOSH model to replicate the storm tide hydrograph shown for Waveland it was necessary to initiate it with a pre-storm water elevation.

Lake Pontchartrain was also rising before the arrival of tropical storm force winds. Figure 9.5 shows the hydrograph for the Mandeville tide gage near the north shore of the lake. Also shown in the figure is the location and distance that the center of Isidore is from the gage. Eventually, Isidore passes directly over the Mandeville gage. The normal lake elevation was a little over one foot above NGVD. It is clear that the lake was gradually rising even when Isidore is located over the Yucatan Peninsula and continued to rise until the storm passed over. For a SLOSH model run to be made in the lake, the initial datum would have to be about 5 feet above NGVD.

SLOSH MODEL RUN AND COMPARISON

The six-hourly track positions, with central pressure and a 70 st mi RMW were used as input data to the SLOSH model runs in the Lake Pontchartrain, Mississippi Sound, Mobile Bay and Pensacola basins. In addition, the hourly locations from the surface pressure analyses and the associated pressure from 0600 UTC to 1800 UTC were also added into the SLOSH runs to override values interpolated from the six-hourly data. The initial water elevation in the Lake Pontchartrain basin was set at 3.1 feet above NGVD for the Gulf of Mexico and 5.0 feet for the lake. The other three basins had lower initial datum and were set accordingly. The astronomical tide level as well as the difference between NGVD and 2002 mean sea level were incorporated into the initial datum. SLOSH model calculated storm surge maximum values were selected at the same locations as the tide gages in Figure 9.3. The comparison is shown in Figure 9.6. Figure 9.7 is the comparison between the observed and SLOSH model hydrographs at Waveland. Figures 9.6 and 9.7 are typical of the comparisons between SLOSH model and observed data when the meteorological input data is known.

Figure 9.8 shows the comparison between the Mandeville observed and SLOSH model hydrographs. The SLOSH model Lake Pontchartrain initial water height essentially remains at 5 feet until the tropical storm arrives and creates a storm surge. It is important to note that the SLOSH model cannot calculate the pre-storm anomaly because it is a Gulf wide phenomenon.

SUMMARY FOR TROPICAL STORM ISIDORE

For tropical storm Isidore, overall, the comparison between the observed and SLOSH model calculated storm surge is good and is typical of the results when the meteorological input is known. The initial water elevations that occurred in Isidore are the largest ever recorded for this area of the coastline and represent a challenge to the operational storm surge specialist.

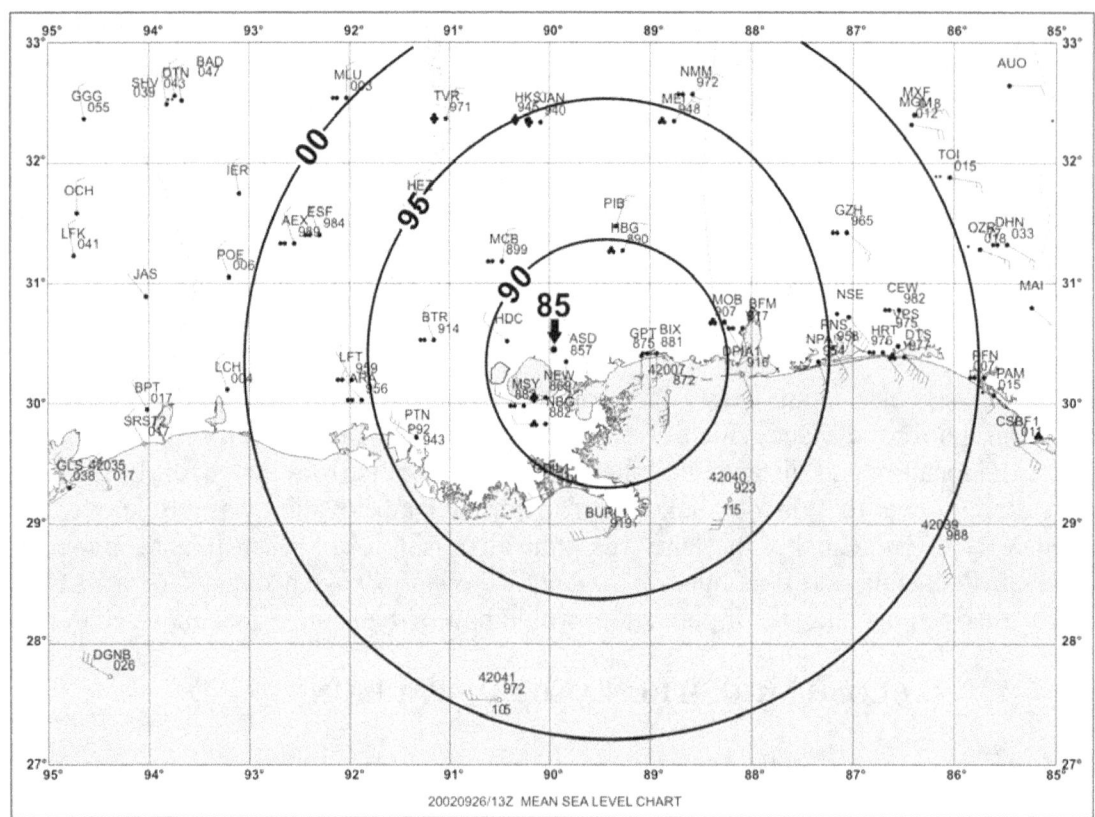

Figure 9.1 Surface pressure analysis for tropical storm Isidore for 1300 UTC on September 26, 2002.

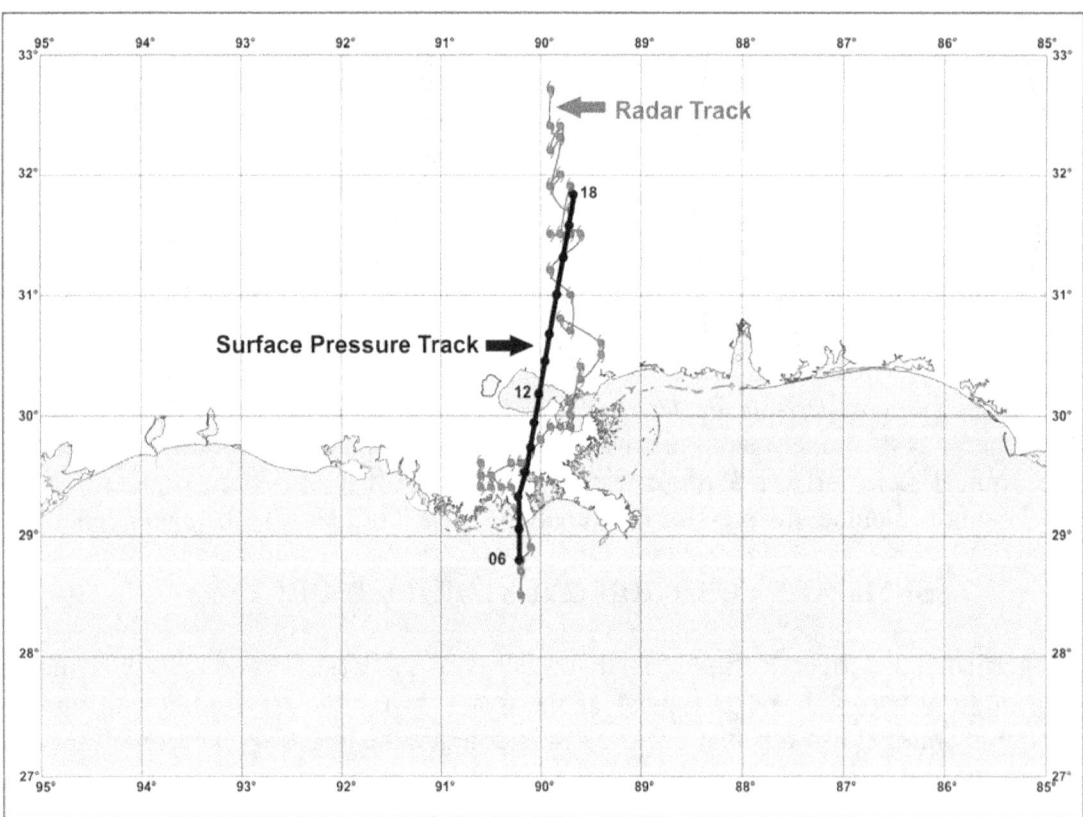

Figure 9.2 Comparison of the tracks from the hourly surface pressure centers (time in UTC) and radar centers for tropical storm Isidore on 26 September 2002.

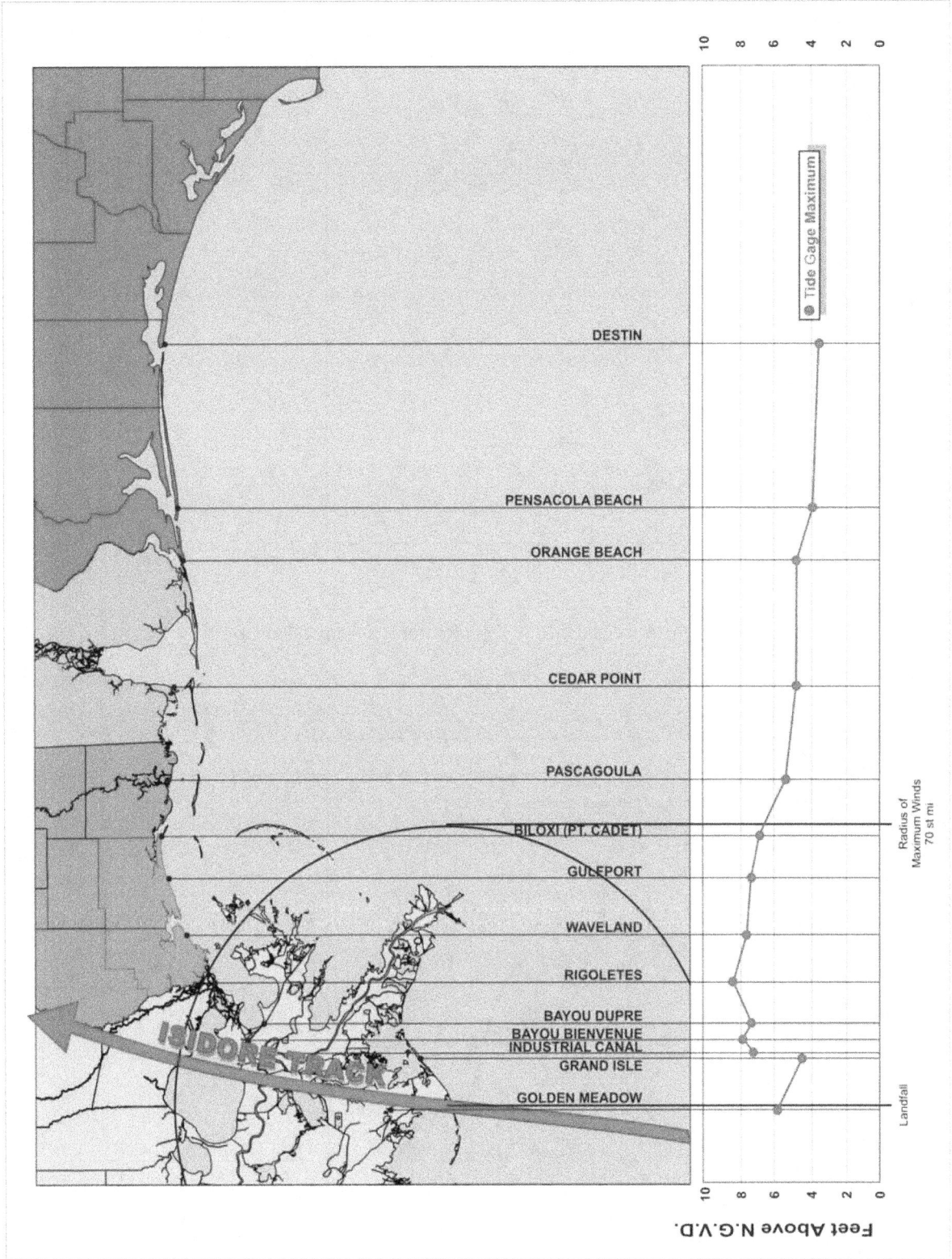

Figure 9.3 Observed coastal storm tide profile for tropical storm Isidore on 26 September 2002.

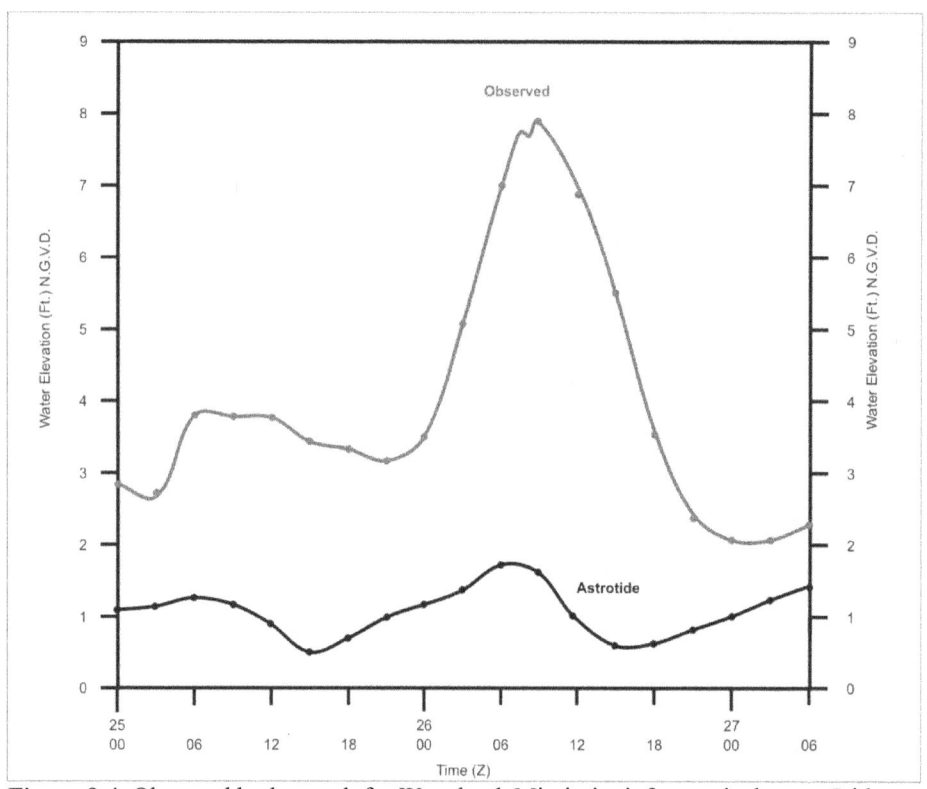

Figure 9.4 Observed hydrograph for Waveland, Mississippi, for tropical storm Isidore, September 18-28, 2002

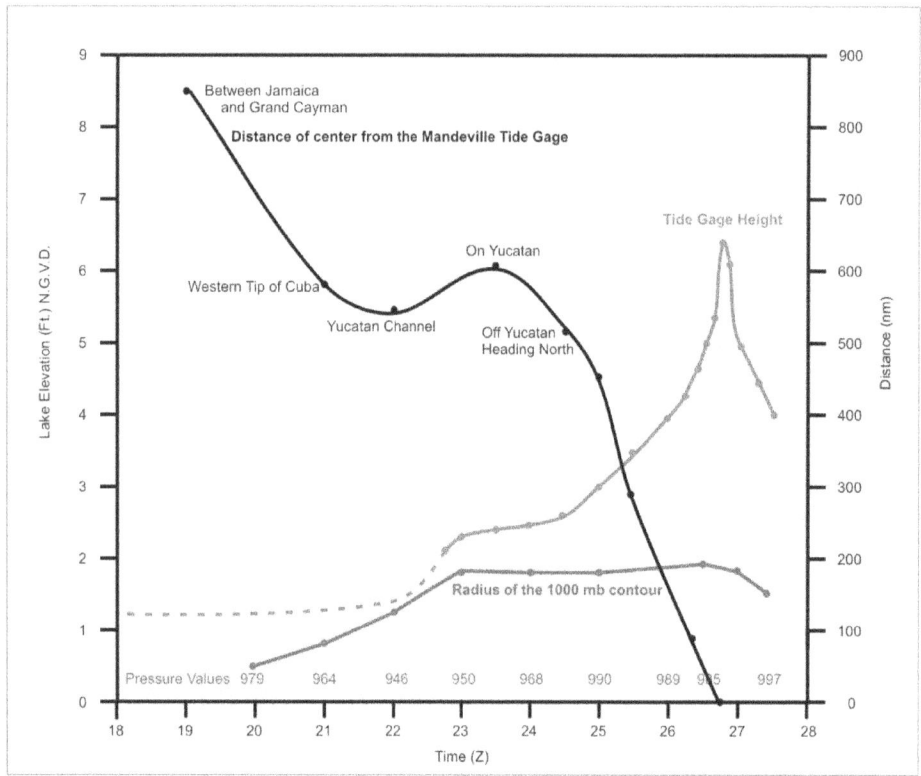

Figure 9.5 Observed hydrograph, distance to storm, storm size and central pressure for Mandeville, Louisiana, for tropical storm Isidore, September 18-28, 2002

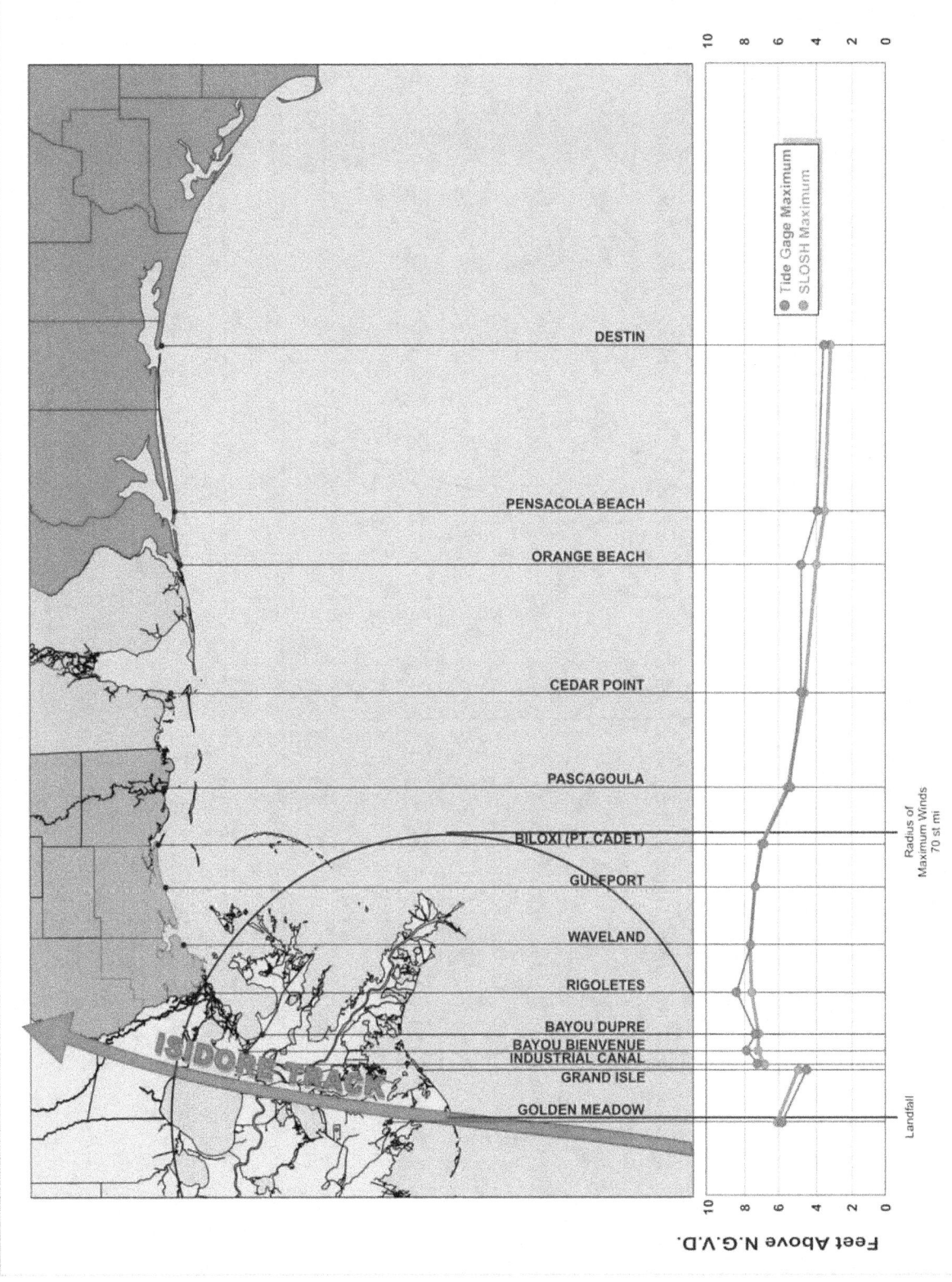

Figure 9.6 Observed coastal and SLOSH model profiles for tropical storm Isidore, on 26 September 2002.

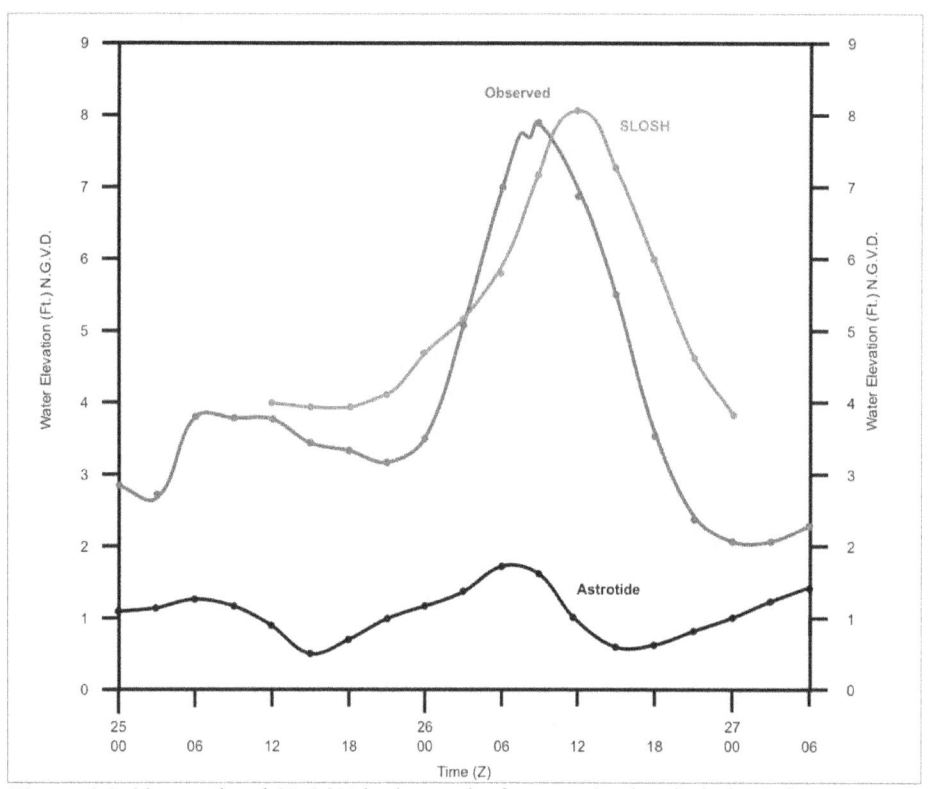

Figure 9.7 Observed and SLOSH hydrographs for Waveland, Mississippi, for tropical storm Isidore, September 25-27, 2002

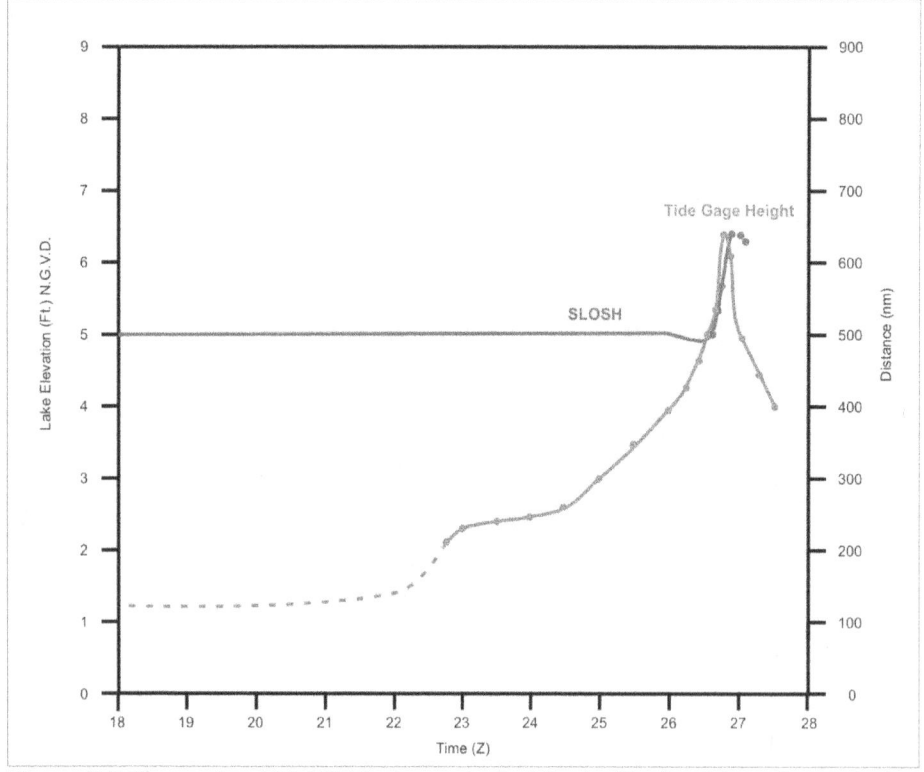

Figure 9.8 Observed and SLOSH hydrographs for Mandeville, Louisiana, for tropical storm Isidore, September 18-28, 2002

SECTION 10

COMPARISON OF OBSERVED AND SLOSH MODEL STORM TIDE IN HURRICANE LILI (2002)

As hurricane Lili approached southern Louisiana it weakened from a category 4 hurricane on the Saffir/Simpson scale to a category 1 at landfall. This is a good example of rapid intensity change just before landfall. Often, along with the intensity change come changes in the size of the wind field. A measure often used to denote this change is the radius of maximum winds (RMW). Both the intensity and the RMW have profound effects on the height and location of the storm surge. Generally, for normal landfalling hurricanes, the maximum storm surge will occur near the location of the RMW on the right side of the center. As a rule, if the RMW remains constant and the intensity decreases, as measured by the central pressure, then the maximum storm surge will decrease. This results because the maximum wind, at this fixed RMW, is decreasing and the total amount of energy going into the water is decreasing. However, if the central pressure remains constant and the RMW is increased the maximum storm surge will increase and its location on the coast will move with the increasing RMW even though the maximum wind speed will decrease. This paradox results because the larger RMW produces a larger wind field (albeit a smaller maximum wind) which in turn has a greater fetch on the water which in turn puts more energy into water over a larger area in the form of waves and currents. Lili is an example of the interplay between these parameters.

METEOROLOGICAL DATA

An excellent summary on the history of this hurricane is given in a report by Lawrence (2003). From the six hourly observations in the report, Lili became a category 4 hurricane in the Gulf of Mexico with a central pressure of 940 mb and a maximum wind speed of 125 kts. The reconnaissance aircraft reported this maximum wind speed about 5 to 6 nautical miles northeast of the center. This is called the primary RMW. During the next 13 hours the central pressure rose, the wind speed decreased and the hurricane made landfall near Intracoastal City, LA. At this time the central pressure was 963 millibars and the maximum wind speed 80 knots. During this same time period a secondary wind maximum formed and was located about 52 nautical miles from the center. This maximum was confirmed by one-minute observations from reconnaissance aircraft as well as estimates from radar. The primary RMW had expanded slightly and was about 9 nautical miles as estimated from radar. However, for storm surge generating potential it is almost inconsequential compared to the much larger 52 nautical mile RMW. Of interest is the fact that standard pressure-wind relationships would give a maximum wind speed of approximately 95 knots for a central pressure of 963 millibars. Many of the pairs of data used to establish these relationships typically had RMW values at 10 to 25 nautical miles. However, when the RMW is large the pressure gradient is spread out and the maximum wind is lower than the standard relationships. This is good for minimizing wind damage potential, but not so for storm surge. Figure 10.1 shows the track of Lili with the primary and secondary RMWs plotted.

HYDROLOGIC DATA

A high water mark survey was conducted by FEMA along the coast of southern Louisiana from just west of Intracoastal City to Grand Isle. Also, the U.S. Army Corps of Engineers, U.S.

Geological Service, National Ocean Service and National Weather Service collected tide gage hydrographs from various locations throughout the region. A coastal profile was created with the tide gage maximums and is also shown in Figure 10.1. In addition, a few high water marks on the western end of the inundated area were also added to supplement the lack of gage maximums. Typically, for a normal land falling hurricane such as Lili the peak storm surge should be near the RMW. In this case it was located near the secondary RMW.

SLOSH MODEL RUN AND COMPARISON

Six-hourly track positions, and central pressure values, obtained from the Lawrence report along with the secondary RMW mentioned above were used as input data to SLOSH model runs in both the Vermilion Bay and Lake Pontchartrain basins (not shown). Also, the initial water elevation used was plus 1.0 feet to account for a small tide anomaly (+0.3 ft) that was occurring before the hurricane arrived and an additional amount for the difference between the sea level elevation in 1929 (NGVD29) and the 2002 mean sea level height (+0.7 ft). No correction was needed for the astronomical tide because it was near mean tide during Lili's landfall. SLOSH model calculated storm surge maximum values were selected at the same locations as the tide gages and high water marks shown in Figure 10.1. The comparison is shown in Figure 10.2. Figure 10.3 shows comparisons between observed tide gage and SLOSH model hydrographs at several locations. Figures 10.2 and 10.3 are typical of the comparisons between SLOSH model and observed data when the meteorological input data is known.

SUMMARY FOR HURRICANE LILI

For hurricane Lili, overall, the comparison between the observed and SLOSH model calculated storm surge is good and is typical of the results when the meteorological input is known. Lili presented a difficult forecast scenario because of the changing size of its wind field when measured by the RMW, as it approached the southern Louisiana coastline.

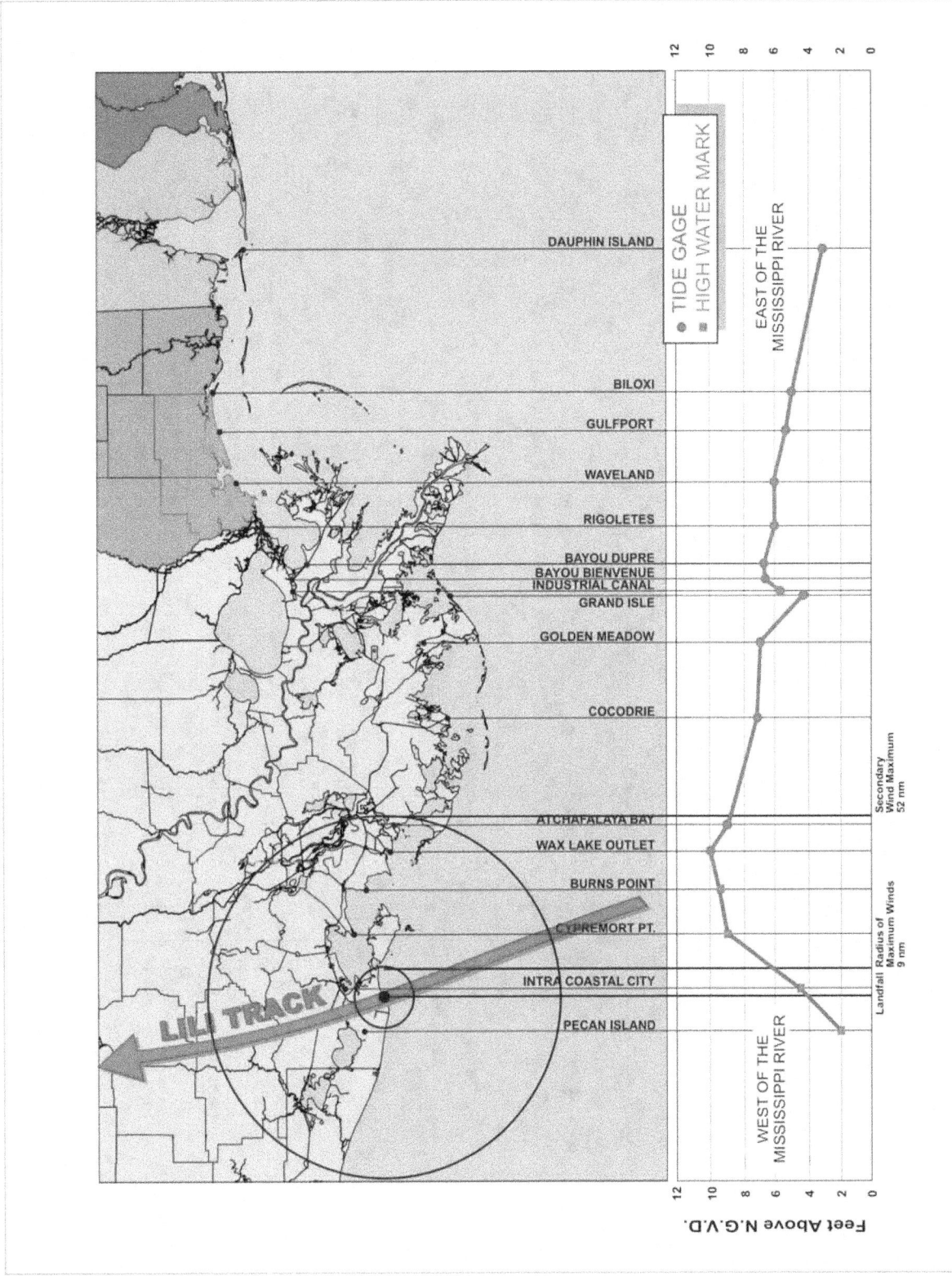

Figure 10.1 Observed coastal storm tide profile for hurricane Lili on October 3, 2002.

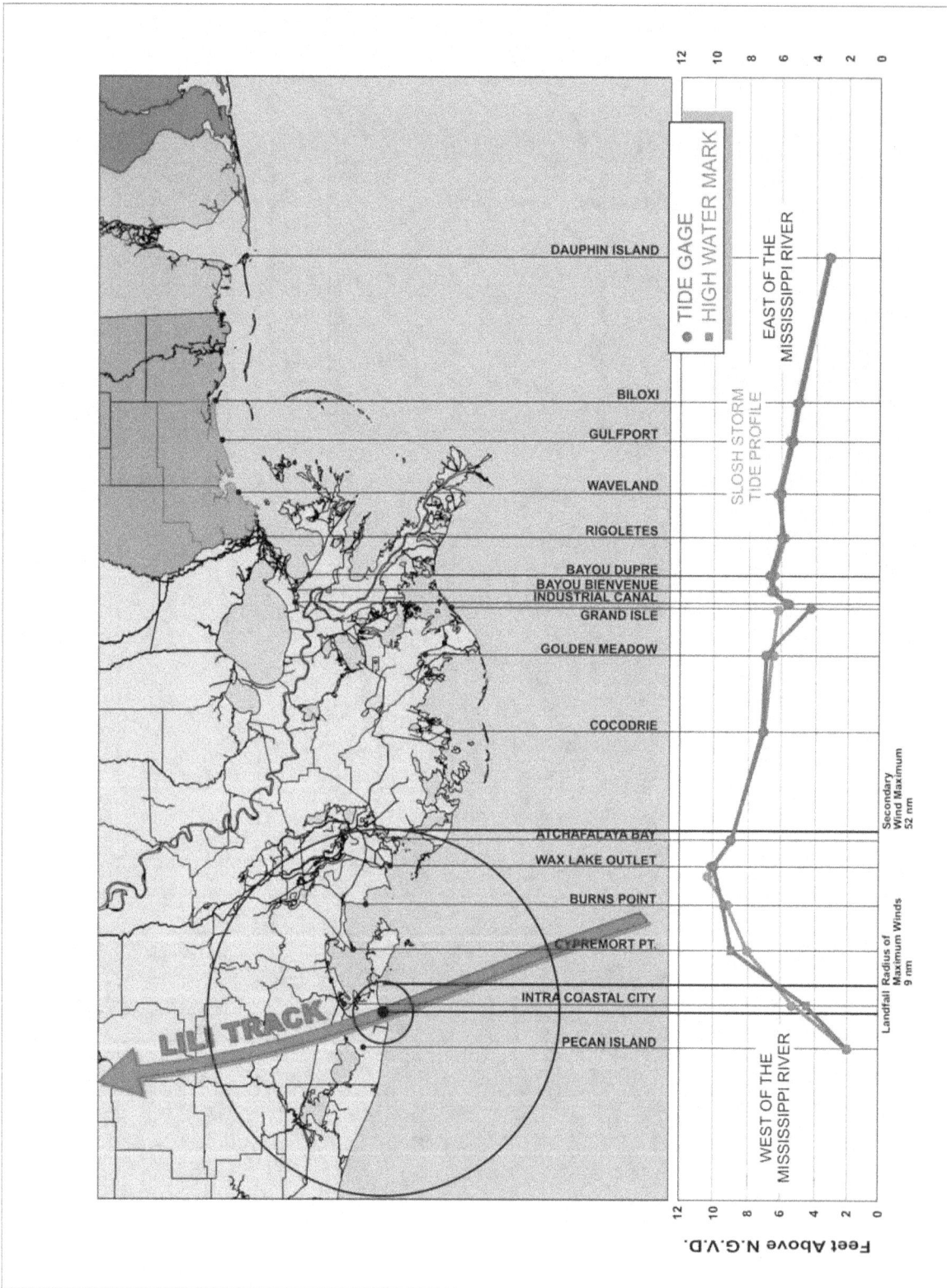

Figure 10.2 Observed and SLOSH coastal storm tide profiles for hurricane Lili on October 3, 2002.

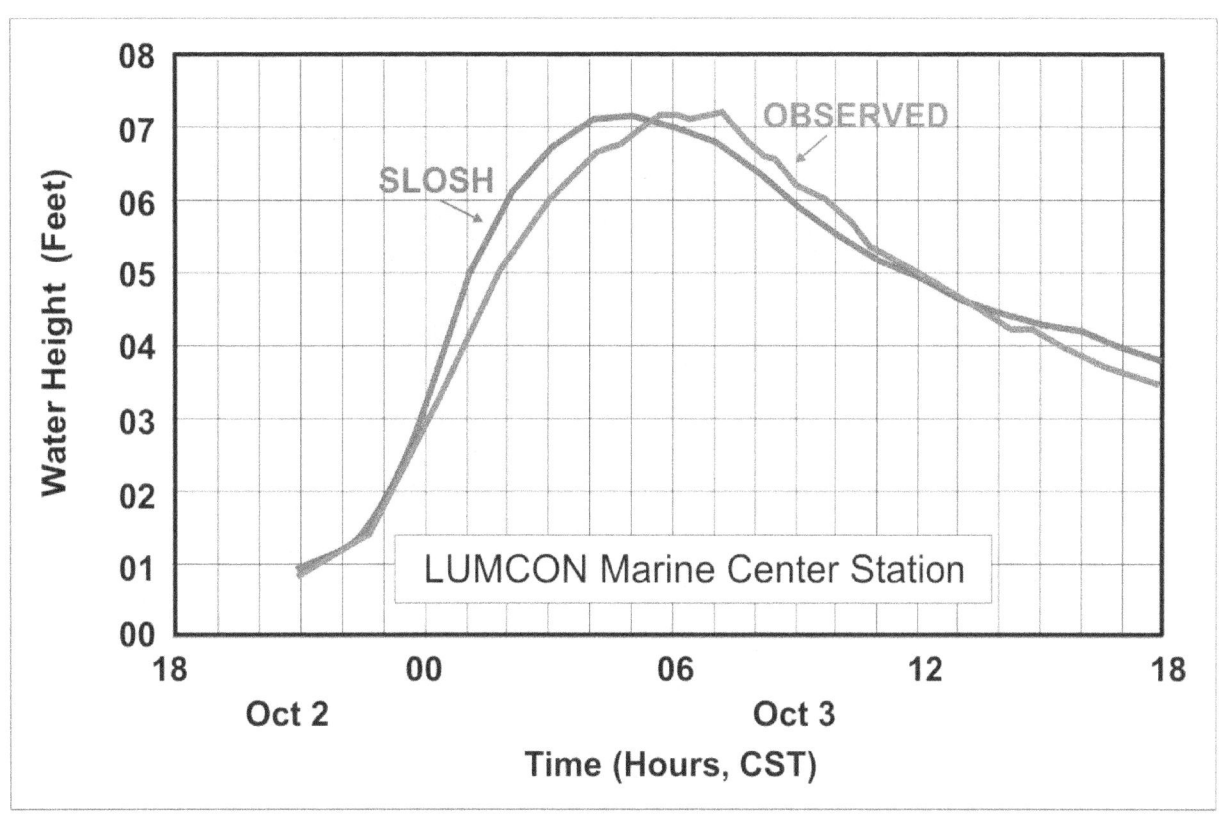

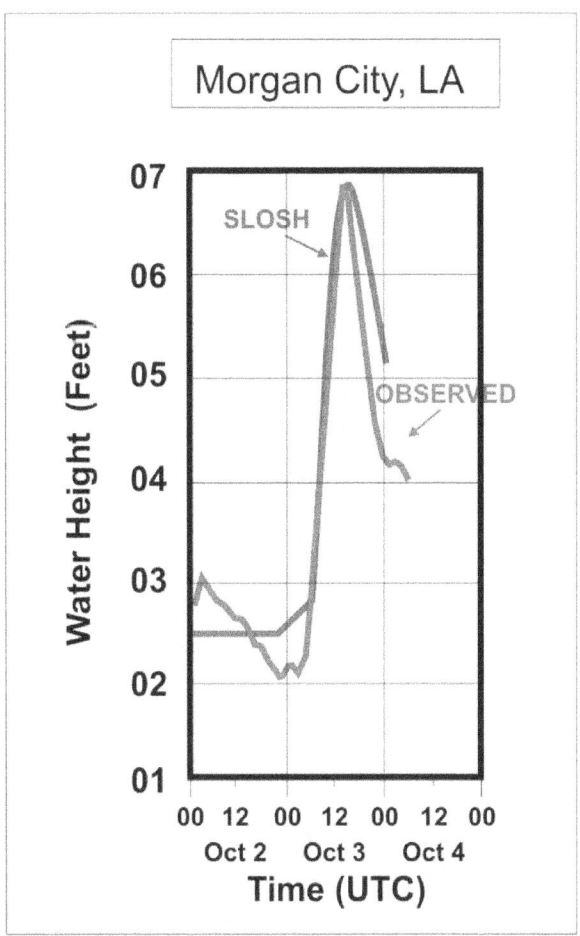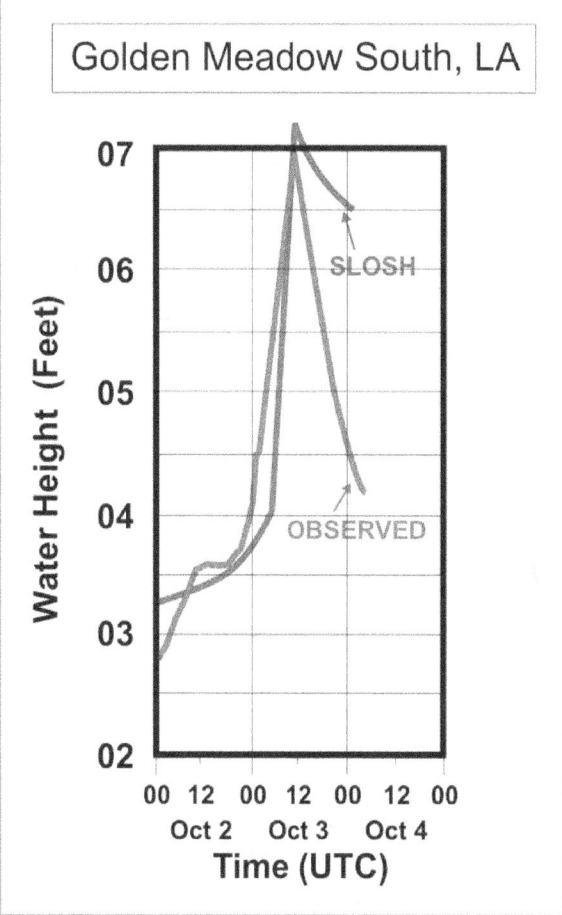

Figure 10.3 Comparison of observed and SLOSH storm tide hydrographs at several locations.

SECTION 11

HURRICANE AUDREY (1957)

Hurricane Audrey was a rare June hurricane that caused approximately 400 deaths in southwest Louisiana. Most of the deaths were due to the storm surge that was generated by a very broad wind field. Surprisingly, the SLOSH model maximum one-minute over the water winds, in this broad wind field were only about 85 to 90 miles per hour. The winds fall within the range of a category 1 on the Saffir Simpson Scale (even though the estimated pressure at landfall was 955 millibars) generated a large and damaging storm surge over a wide area.

The two dimensional extent of the storm surge was impressive. It extended along all of the Texas and Louisiana coasts and a portion of the Mississippi coast. Water elevations of 5 feet or higher were observed from just south of Freeport, Texas eastward to Cocodrie, Louisiana- a coastal distance of approximately of 310 statute miles. In Louisiana the storm surge spread 10 to 30 statute miles inland east of where the center made landfall. Much of this area is marsh land with elevations of only a few feet above sea level. The area is also punctuated by low ridgelines running east to west called cheniers. The cheniers are the remnants of ancient shorelines. They are largely composed of sand and almost all are located inland from the Gulf of Mexico shoreline. Most of the small towns and individual homes in this area are built on the cheniers.

METEOROLOGICAL DATA

Two good summaries of the history of the hurricane are given by Moore and Staff (1957) and Ross and Blum (1957). A summary of some of their observations follows:

1. Audrey formed in the Bay of Campeche on June 24, from an easterly wave.
2. The central pressure values and wind values from reconnaissance for the next 2 days are; June 25, 989 millibars and 85 knots; June 25, 979 millibars and 75 knots June 26, 973 millibars and 90 knots. No more reconnaissance eye penetrations were made but eye positions from radar were given and wind observations around the hurricane were taken. Eye positions were also determined from the land based radar at Lake Charles, Louisiana. The highest wind observation from the reconnaissance was reported just as the eye was making landfall. It was 95 knots and the aircraft was located 110 nautical miles southeast of the center. The last reliable pressure before landfall was taken by the Tanker Tillamook on June 27 at approximately 0400 Central Standard Time. It was about 21 nautical miles west of the track and reported a pressure of 969 millibars.
3. Land station minimum pressure values were: Lake Charles, Louisiana, 972 millibars; Port Arthur, Texas, 966 millibars; Calcasieu Coast Guard Station, Louisiana, 960 millibars; Cameron, Louisiana, 959 millibars; and Hackberry, Louisiana, 958 millibars.
4. The only reliable wind observations were the reconnaissance values given above and two reports from land locations. One from Orange, Texas reported winds over 100 miles per hour just before a dead calm. The other was from Lake Charles, Louisiana which reported winds of 105 miles per hour. The two land reports do not define the wind as either sustained or gust. It is possible that these are observed wind speed maximums as seen on a dial and may be gusts.
5. The hurricane moved northward and gradually picked up forward speed. It made landfall at the coast moving about 14 miles per hour.

6. No quantitative information is given on the size of the hurricane. The Moore and Staff report states that the Tanker Tillamook, mentioned above, "was in the western portion of the eye and that the pressure observed was not the absolute minimum in the center at that time". Thus, the RMW on the west side must be greater than 21 nautical miles. Qualitatively, the reports suggest a hurricane growing in size as it approached the coast.

HYDROLOGIC DATA

As part of the National Hurricane Research Project Harris (1958) produced a report on the storm tide produced by Audrey. The report included maps with the location and value of high water marks taken in the post hurricane survey and storm tide hydrographs obtained from numerous tide gages in the region. The large amount of data would require months of analysis and verification and is beyond the scope of this report. But a series of storm tide hydrographs from gages located in strategic locations will be compared to SLOSH/TIDE model hydrographs.

A coastal profile appeared in the Moore and Staff article and was found to have an error in the distances on the left side of the hurricane. It was re-plotted for this report and was compared to the SLOSH model generated coastal profile.

DISCUSSION

The hourly track positions of Audrey are shown in figure 11.1. These were determined from radar center fixes, the Tillamook observation and an analysis of the surface pressure values on land. The surface pressure values and analysis gave an estimated 955 millibar pressure value at landfall. The hurricane was moving northward at about 14 miles per hour at landfall.

Two scenarios exist for the development of this hurricane from noon on June 26, when the last pressure observation of 973 millibars was measured from the reconnaissance flight and landfall the next morning with a pressure of 955 millibars. The first is a steadily deepening hurricane that reaches it lowest pressure at landfall. This is supported by the central pressure values from the reconnaissance flights and the ship report which reported about 4 to 5 hours before landfall. Figure 11.2 is a plot of central pressure versus time with the observed pressure noted. The dashed line labeled Scenario 1 represents an approximate linear deepening rate of about one millibar per hour until landfall. The ship was located about 21 nautical miles to the west of the center of the hurricane as it passed by. Its value of 969 millibars could be used to extrapolate a central pressure value of 960 millibars. In the remaining hours until landfall the hurricane would have deepened to 955 millibars.

The second scenario was created by Moore and Staff and is the one currently recorded in the best track data file maintained at the National Hurricane Center. Their reasoning is that after the last reconnaissance flight on June 26, the hurricane deepened rapidly down to 943 millibars and maintained this until landfall. They support this by observations from the pressure and maximum wind observations from an oil rig (925 millibars and 180 miles per hour) and four sea tenders in the hurricane (winds greater than 100 miles per hour with the three nearest the center reporting winds of 140 to 150 miles per hour). All of these sensors were elevated and not calibrated. Generally, rapid deepening is associated with a small RMW of 5 to 15 statute miles. The observation from the Tillamook tends to suggest otherwise, since it appears to be in the western part of the eye. Their scenario is labeled in Figure 11.2 as Scenario 2.

The most difficult parameter to determine is the Radius of Maximum Winds (RMW). The Tillamook location and observations suggests at least a 30 nautical miles (35 statute miles) RMW on the west side of the hurricane. Generally, for a normal land falling hurricane, the highest storm tide values occur on the right hand side where the RMW is located. In this case, it is about 35 statute miles to the east of the center based upon the observations. But, the coastal configuration where Audrey made landfall has a concave shape. This tends to funnel water toward the back of the concave and the high storm tide values would tend to be nearer this location. So the RMW could be larger than 35 statute miles. Finally, the storm tide heights measured at Galveston and Freeport, located to the west of the eye landfall, suggest a large RMW that pushes water toward the west well ahead of the center passage.

SLOSH MODEL SIMULATION

Harris points out that almost all of the tide gages in the region were running about one to one and one-half feet above normal before Audrey made landfall. This was a pre-storm tide anomaly and +1.3 was used to take this into account. In addition, an adjustment was made for high tide (+0.5 feet) and a correction made for the difference between mean sea level and NGVD (+0.2 feet). Thus, the initial water elevation was set at +2.0 feet.

Scenario one above is the one used for this SLOSH simulation. The values in Figure 11.1 were used as input parameters. SLOSH model simulations were made with varying RMWs. A RMW of 60 statute miles produced the best results. Figure 11.1 shows a circle which represents the location of the maximum winds and on the circle is a wind vector showing the wind direction and the maximum wind speed of 87 miles per hour. Also shown is the radius of 60 statute miles.

Figure 11.3 is a comparison between the observed coastal and SLOSH/TIDE model storm tide profiles. The SLOSH/TIDE profile is slightly below the observed profile which may reflect some additional water elevation in the high water marks due to breaking waves. Many of the locations where the highest observations were taken are located on cheniers. The cheniers, as mentioned above, are located back from the coast and are fronted by marsh land that is generally 1 to 3 feet above sea level. As the storm surge rose and covered the marsh land, the cheniers became the "new beach". The water continued to rise and then supported waves that broke on the structures on the cheniers. Not unexpectedly, most of the highest water observations were recorded on the cheniers closest to the Gulf of Mexico.

Five tide gage hydrographs from Harris are of particular interest and are shown in Figure 11.4. Four (Lake Charles, North Lake Calcasieu, Hackberry, and Cameron) show how the storm surge penetrated inland over a distance of 35 miles and the fifth one (Pecan Island) shows the effect of a chenier acting as barrier to the storm tide until it is overtopped. Also plotted are the SLOSH model hydrographs at the same locations for comparison purposes. The first four hydrographs extend from Cameron to Lake Charles and the locations where they were recorded are shown in Figure 11.1. At Cameron the observed hydrograph was actually created from eye witness accounts of the rising water and a high water mark taken after the hurricane. There may be timing issues with this hydrograph and that may be the reason that the SLOSH maximum and observed maximum are about four and one-half hours apart. The Hackberry hydrograph is next and the comparison is good except the SLOSH model is high. At both North Lake Calcasieu and Lake Charles the comparisons are good. The observed hydrographs showed that the peak storm surge took about 6 to 7 hours to move from Cameron to Lake Charles. The peak storm surges at Hackberry, North Lake Calcasieu and Lake Charles were 6.7, 7.7 and 7.0 feet respectively. Note that the surges are not decreasing but remaining approximately the same as it moves inland. This should effectively end the myth regarding marshes decreasing the surge as you move inland. But a person might ask, "Since the value at Cameron was 12.1 feet, didn't a decrease occur?" Cameron is located on a chenier, which means the water must first pile up and overtop it before it can continue to move inland. If the chenier was not present, the water would not have piled up to the heights observed and higher water elevations would have been observed at the Hackberry, North Lake Calcasieu and Lake Charles. Except for the comparison at Cameron the SLOSH model does a good job of reproducing the surges inland but is a little higher than observed.

The tide gage at Pecan Island is very interesting. The gage was located on the south side of White Lake and behind or on the north side of a chenier that is unusually high at 11 to 12 feet in elevation. As the hurricane approached, the strong easterly and southeasterly winds drove the water in the lake toward the west and the water level went down on the eastern side where the gage was located. The storm surge rose on the outer coast, moved inland over the marsh and piled up on the south side of the chenier to an observed elevation of 10.5 feet. This was not enough to overtop it. Meanwhile, the storm surge east and west of Pecan Island was over-topping the chenier where the heights were lower. The water moved rapidly to where the gage was and the rise is evident in the hydrograph. The SLOSH model does not show the initial fall in the water level but captures some of the rapid rise and the peak values.

Overall the SLOSH model simulates much of what happened with the storm surge during hurricane Audrey. In order to produce such a wide spread storm surge the hurricane must have had a large RMW. This compares quite well with Lili's (see Section 10) large RMW at landfall.

If we run the SLOSH model with the parameters using Scenario 2, the hurricane is steadily deepened to 943 at landfall. A smaller RMW of 30 statute miles is used to account for the observation from the Tillamook. A SLOSH model run was made with these parameters and a disaster far worse than what occurred would have taken place. For example, the maximums near Cameron and eastward on Figure 11.3 would increase to over 15 feet and the maximum storm surge values at Hackberry, North Lake Calcasieu and Lake Charles would be 13.0, 13.6 and 13.9 feet respectively or almost double what was observed. The SLOSH value at Galveston would have been reduced to 3.3 feet. Scenario 2 is not what actually occurred.

SUMMARY FOR HURRICANE AUDREY

Hurricane Audrey was a category 1 hurricane at landfall when one uses the wind speed as a measure of intensity. However, the central pressure was 955 millibars which usually indicates a category 3. The large RMW of 60 statute miles produced a broad wind field that put a greater amount of energy into the storm surge compared to a climatologically average RMW of 15 to 25 statute miles. This resulted in a storm surge over a long span of the Gulf of Mexico coastline. This same dilemma occurred recently in hurricane Katrina (2005) where the central pressure at landfall on the Mississippi coast was 930 millibars (category 4 pressure) but a RMW of 40 statute miles produced a broad pressure gradient that gave category 2 winds. However, this combination of low pressure and large RMW in Katrina produced a record U.S. storm surge of approximately 25 to 26 feet.

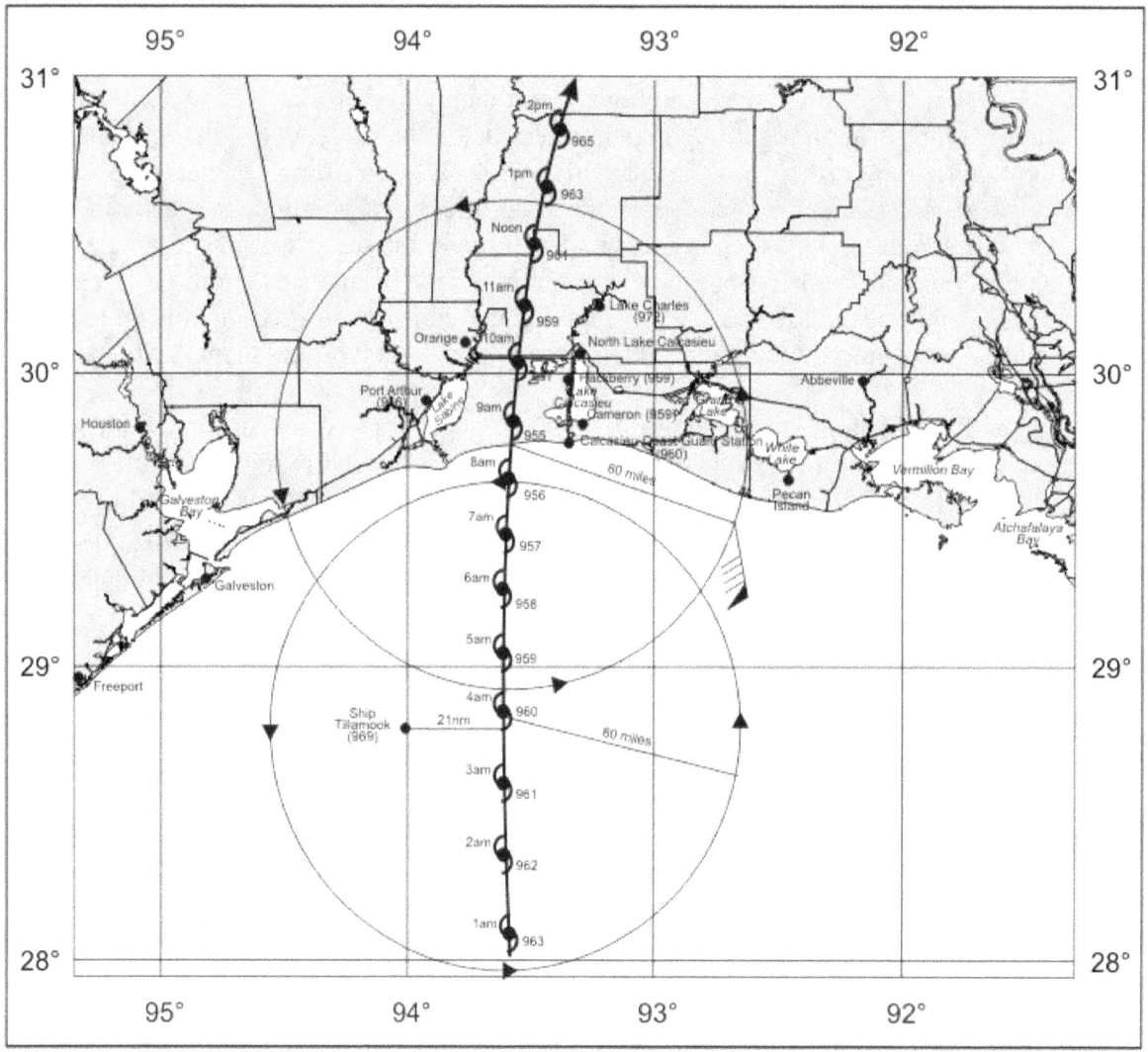

Figure 11.1 Track of hurricane Audrey for June 27, 1957. Hourly positions are labeled in Local Standard Time and pressure in millibars. Circles with radial distance of 60 statute miles are the location of the maximum winds. Wind vectors in miles per hour.

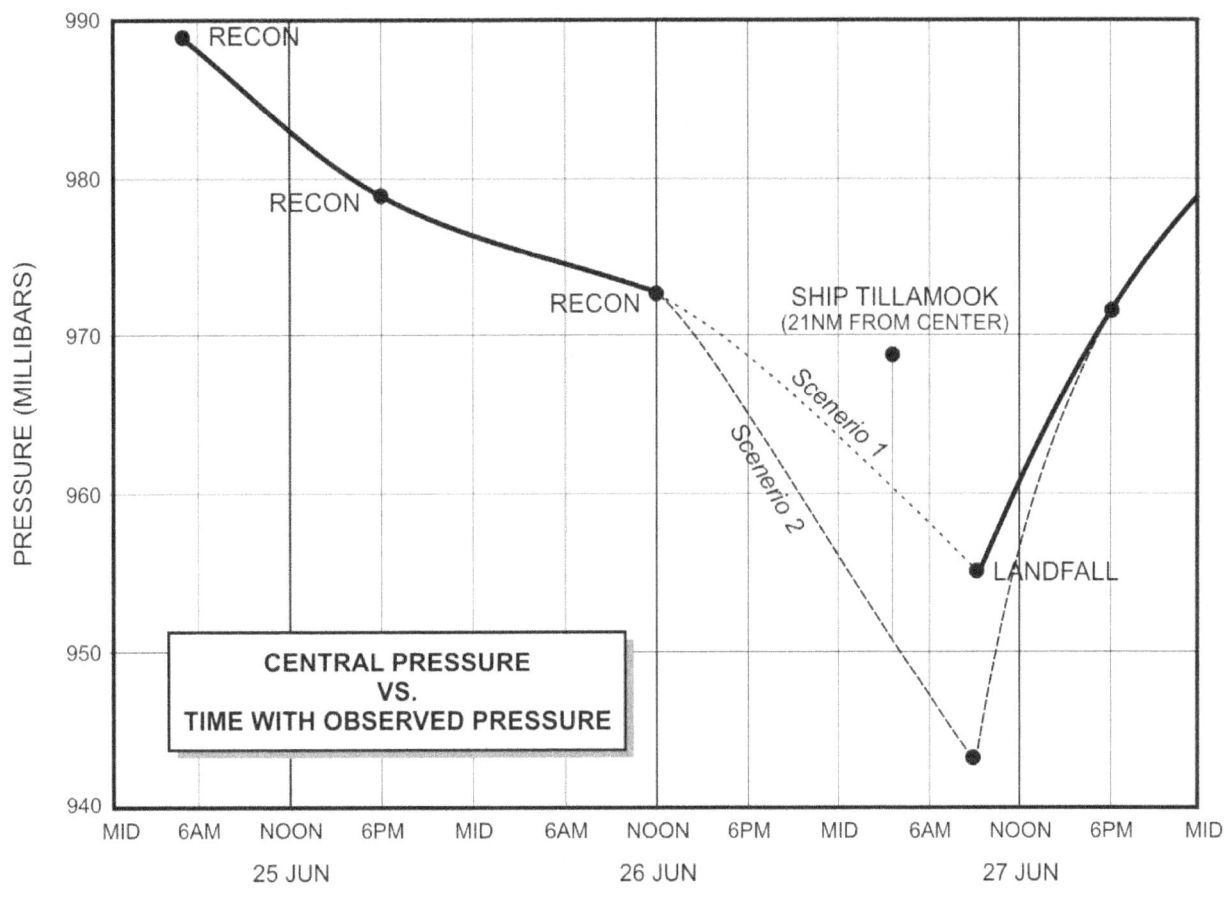

Figure 11.2 Plot of central pressure vs. time with observed pressure noted. Dashed lines represent two deepening scenarios.

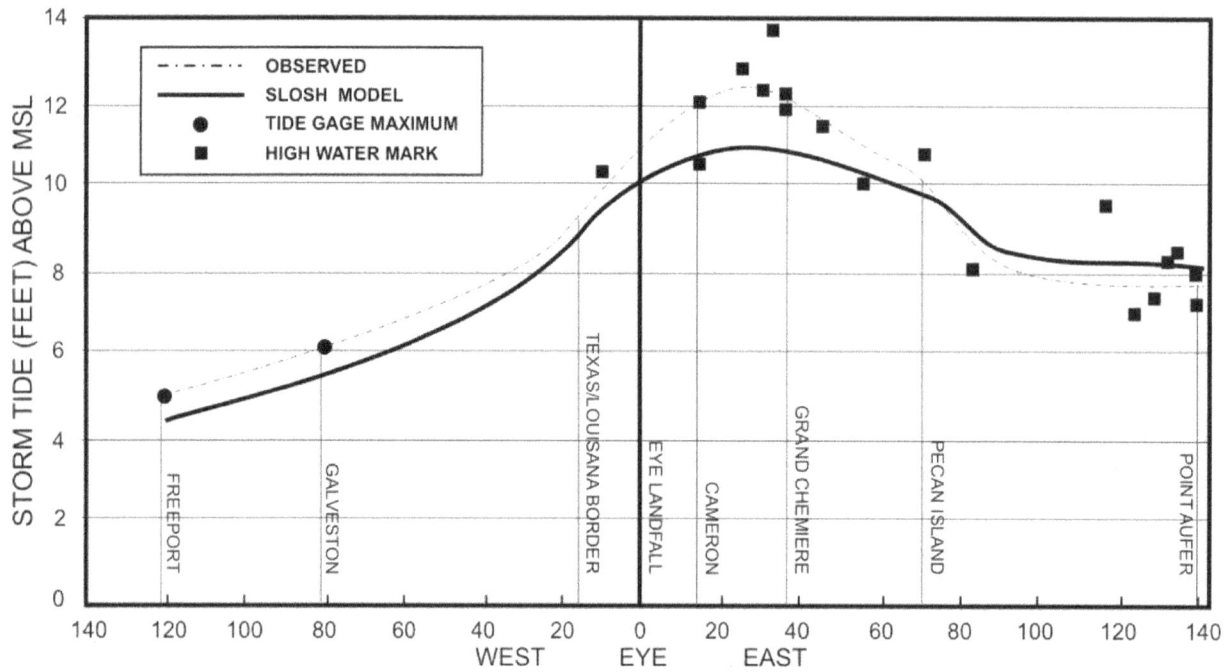

Figure 11.3 Plot of observed high water marks and tide gage maximums for hurricane Audrey. Comparison of observed and SLOSH/Tide model coastal profiles in feet above mean sea level.

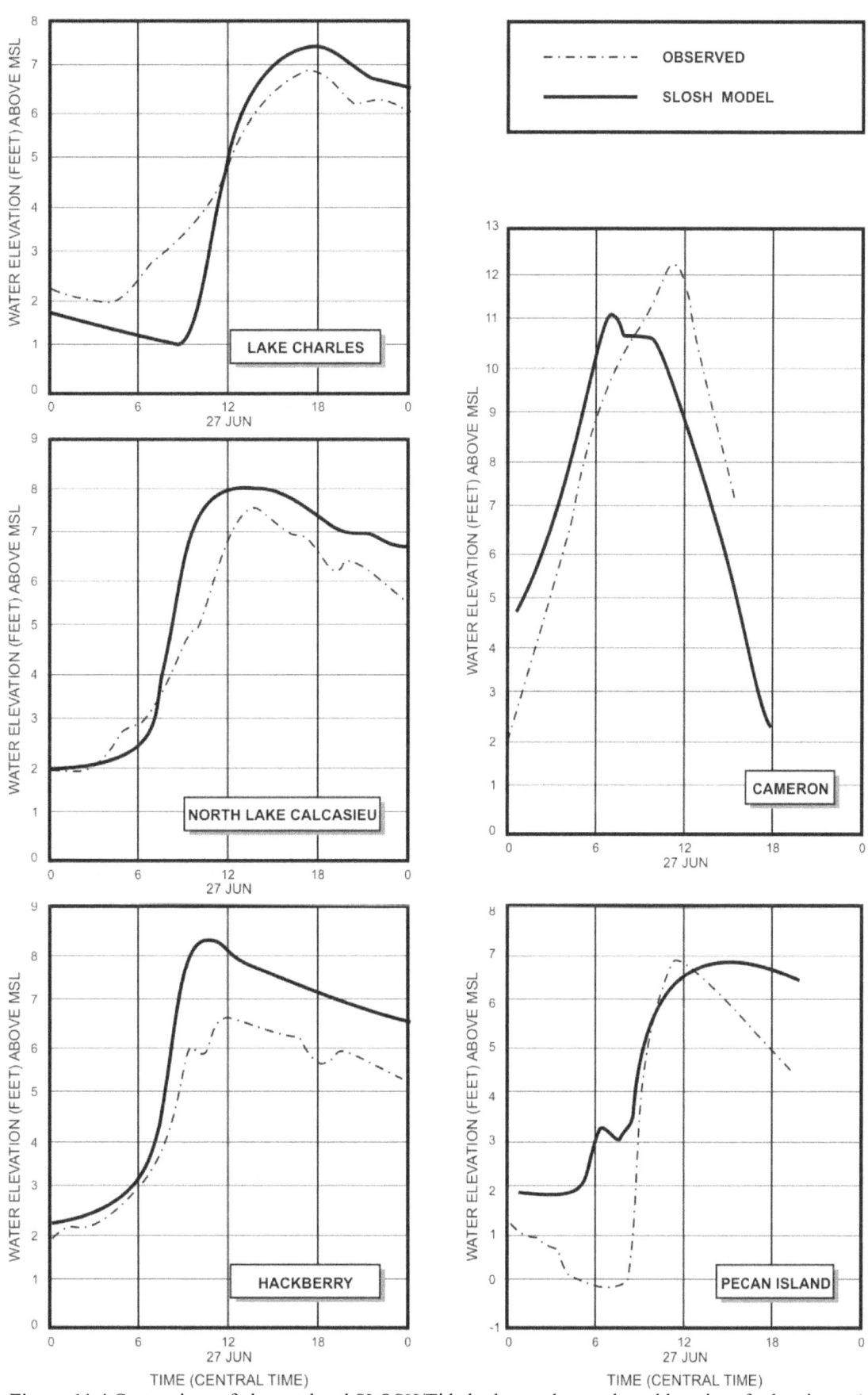

Figure 11.4 Comparison of observed and SLOSH/Tide hydrographs at selected locations for hurricane Audrey.

THE 1900 GALVESTON HURRICANE

This hurricane caused the greatest loss of life due to storm surge in U.S. history. This is another case of coastal development on a low barrier island in a highly vulnerable location for hurricane storm surge. Contrary to what might be expected, the maximum storm surge elevation on Galveston Island was only about 12 feet above sea level. However, large breaking waves riding on top of the storm surge caused most of the lost structures to move from their foundations and break up. Locations on Galveston Island that were low and thinly populated with structures were swept clean and much of the debris was carried by the storm surge to the mainland. Interspersed with the other debris were the bodies of the victims, both human and animal, that did not survive the storm. In the part of the island that was more densely populated and somewhat higher, the storm surge was not present long enough to sweep everything from the island. In this area a wall of debris composed of destroyed buildings slowly moved onto the island like a steam roller, and knocked over other buildings. This wall of debris prevented the breaking waves from impacting structures closer to the center of the city. They still got storm surge generated water in them, but without the additional breaking wave damage. In these structures the water generally rose up without agitation and the people in them sought to keep their heads above water. For the inhabitants caught up in the debris field it was a struggle to survive against all the deadly forces of the hurricane. These forces included breaking waves on top of the storm surge which tossed and turned the debris, wind-borne debris flying through the air, and the stinging effects of wind driven rain and sea spray which made it difficult to breathe. Many people were crushed and drowned in the churning debris and many were probably knocked unconscious by the flying missiles and then drowned. In the debris field, which acted like a flexible dam, the breaking waves added to the total water elevation. The rapid "up rush" of water, as reported by many survivors, is an indication of the breaking wave effect. This additional water height would "leak through" and add to storm surge elevations in structures immediately on the landward side of the debris field. This is well documented by Issac Cline in his account of events during the hurricane. In this paper, a comparison of Cline's estimation of the water elevations with time and the SLOSH model hydrograph for the same location will be made.

METEOROLOGICAL DATA

The Monthly Weather Review article by E. B. Garriot (1900) gives a summary of all data that was immediately available after the hurricane. Twelve-hourly surface wind and pressure observations, available from the National Climate Data Center in Asheville, NC, for selected stations along the Gulf of Mexico coastline, including a few ship reports, allow for a track analysis of the system as it moves across the Gulf from near Florida to Texas. Additional data was found by Mr. Lew Fincher, a historical hurricane researcher. These include the following excerpts from several documents:

1. "THE GREAT GALVESTON DISASTER" by Paul Lester.

"The town of Alvin was practically demolished. Hitchcock suffered severely from the storm, while the little town of Alta Loma is reported without a house standing. The town of Pearl has lost one-half of its buildings. The Santa Fe train which left here at 7:55 Saturday night, 8th (of September) was wrecked at a point about two miles north of Alvin. The train was running slowly when it encountered the heavy storm. It is reported that the train was literally lifted from the track. Advancing inland, the storm swept into Hempstead, 50 miles above Houston, thence to Chapell Hill 20 miles further; thence to Brenham, 30 miles further, wrecking all 3 towns. Several persons were killed.

Captain Falfor, of the U. S. Engineers Corps, during the hurricane was at Quintana, at the mouth of the Brazos River, where he has been supervising Government works. He stated today that the Barometer fell to 27.60, and the wind velocity was one hundred and twenty miles an hour. Fifty-four houses were wrecked in Quintana and the debris piled up in the streets. Fortunately no lives were lost.

The town of Velasco, three miles above (Quintana), on the east side of the river, was completely wrecked. Nine persons were killed, three in the hotel, which was badly demolished. Angleton, the county seat of Bazoria, ten miles north of Velasco was almost completely destroyed. Several lives were lost and a number of persons badly injured."

2. From "The Autobiography of Benjamin Hardy Carlton, MD" (1938)

"The year was 1900. On September 5th (Editor's note: Actually it was September 7th.), the wind was blowing from the north and the water was rising. I consulted the old settlers of Quintana, asking them if it wasn't a storm coming. They said no, it was impossible to have a storm with the wind coming from the north. Well, I wondered what was going to happen. The wind was getting stronger and stronger and the tide was inundating the lower part of town. If it continues like that, what are you going to call it? At that time, we had two homes, one in Quintana and another in Velasco. On September 6th (actually the 7th), I went to Velasco to attend the Masonic Lodge, taking with me my wife and my two small daughters, Doris and Myrtle. I left the two boys, Marion and Columbus at Quintana. After the close of the meeting I took a sick headache which I had periodically for a number of years. We decided to stay overnight with my brother-in-law, C. C. Johnson.

The next morning (September 8, 8 AM) the wind was stronger than ever and I attempted to go back to Quintana. Reaching about half the distance I discovered that the water was all over the prairie and floating logs made it impossible to go on. By the time I got back to Velasco the river had become so rough that the ferryboat could not operate. There were two government boats anchored in the river so I asked the officers if they couldn't go down to Quintana and reach my sons and the other folks that were there. They said they would take great pleasure in doing anything for me they could and immediately began to get steam up. I sent word to Lena that if the storm increased, not to attempt to go to the Velasco hotel as I considered it unsafe, but just to remain in our home.

Upon arriving at Quintana they attempted to anchor the steamboat just opposite the lighthouse. They threw ropes over the piling and it snapped like a pipe stem. The boat was drifting rapidly out towards the gulf. The captain turned into the wind and put on all the steam they had. Throwing out the anchors they finally brought the boat to a standstill. The captain ordered his men to get me ashore in a lifeboat. Arriving on shore I found that everything in the lower part of town was under water. I met my son, Columbus, telling him to stay in a certain house nearby. I had my boatman take the quarantine boat and help to remove his family, including a baby just several days old. When we got there, water was up to the door. After getting them to the boat we proceeded to try and reach higher ground. We hadn't gotten far when the boat swamped. I was holding the little baby and trying to walk with the wind in waist deep water. Every thirty or forty feet the wind would blow me down…the baby being completely immersed each time.   I finally reached Captain Bowers house completely exhausted, but I still had the baby. I expected that the baby had not survived the ordeal but when I unwrapped it, it was sound asleep.

The mother and father with several others were fortunate to reach higher ground. In the excitement they lost one little boy but later found him clinging to the branches of a salt cedar unharmed. At this time most of the houses were being blown away and Captain Bowers' house was a two story one. Near his house was a one-story house that was supposed to be storm proof that was built by a syndicate during the construction of the jetties. Thinking that the Bowers house would soon collapse, we made several attempts to reach the other house.   When we were about to make a dash for it we looked out and the house was gone. We went back upstairs and shortly afterwards a two by four was blown through the double walls, through a double partition, and into the piano.

Soon after, a lull came and there was not a breath of air. I tried to reach the baby's mother and father to tell them that their baby was safe. On the way the water was up to my chin. They were very happy to learn that their baby was safe. The lull lasted for about 15 minutes, and then the wind came back from the south at the same velocity that it had been coming from the north. Amazingly, my watch, which had been immersed in the water several times, was still running. It and the clock on the wall both said 8:10 PM. We had all gone through so much, it felt like it should be about twelve o'clock. There I was and I did not know if any of my family was living or not." (Editor's note: His family had all survived.)

3. Letter from Miss Earel L. Brunner, written Ada, Oklahoma on May 22, 1950, to Mr. W. M. Quillin of Greenville, Tennessee.

"The 1900 Galveston storm started on a still, foggy morning. By evening it was drizzling. Next day, it was raining with a breeze. It blew harder as the day advance and next day it was scary. By that night the milk house blew away, the porch roof blew in two in the middle and swapped ends. We got busy nailing braces up stairs and down where walls heaved in and out.

Pretty soon, the north east upstairs window blew out, letting the wind in the house. It ripped through the roof just above the window and burst the south west corner of the house from roof to the foundation from which it moved it.

We were convinced then, it was time to leave the house. A south east window was kicked out and we began to get out. Father, J. D. Brunner, placed me, Earel, on the ground some distance from the house, with one arm around the fence post, my oldest brother, Forest, in my lap and a quilt around both of us. Uncle Robin, R. L. Bounds, took my baby brother, Hayden the same way at another post. Father left me and crawled back to the house to get mother, but she had already stepped out the window before he got there. The instant she stepped out, the wind snatched her quilt and the next thing she knew, she was on the other side of a six foot net wire fence, headed toward a lake just beyond. She grabbed a wagon as she passed and held on for dear life. The wagon would tip on two wheels and threaten to turn over with her. Father kept crawling, calling and searching for her all during the storm, but his voice was blotted out by the terrible thunder and lightning and the roar of the wind and rain that hammered like sleet. It seemed in the lightning flashes that one tunnel or column of water would chase another as the great gusts of wind nearly made typhoons of them. This lasted till midnight. Then it became a clear, calm night just as if nothing had happened.

In the moonlight we saw the crazily leaning house. We knew better than to try and spend the rest of the night in it. The water was perhaps six inches deep all over the yard, and we were soaking wet. So were the matches and wood. No fire to get dry by.

We dragged out some wet mattresses, built a platform to place them on, nailed up a hurried shelter out of planks for a temporary shelter and the storm came back. After that hour of calm, clear moonlight, it just blew as hard from the southwest as it did from the northeast.

This straightened the house up a little, but it tightened the stairway that had been pulled away from the wall down on some feather pillows and feather beds that were blown in there. They had to be cut off to save them at all.

Next day, when we checked up on the damage, we were too discouraged to even think of trying to rebuild again there, but began trying to figure out how to get away. No money, and every crop a total loss. The barns, chicken houses, milk house and both homes either gone or total wrecks." (Editor's note: Within a year, the family left and moved back to Oklahoma.)

HYDROLOGIC DATA

Mr. Bill Read, Meteorologist in Charge, of the National Weather Service Office in Houston/Galveston, Texas supplied a record of high water marks for historical hurricanes that were recorded at a church in downtown Galveston. The record begins with the 1900 hurricane and ends with hurricane Alicia in 1983. The value for the 1900 hurricane is 11.7 feet above mean sea level. Interestingly, the highest value is 12.3 feet recorded in the 1915 hurricane which will be discussed in the next section.

Besides the account of the water elevation at Quintana mentioned in Dr. Carlton's autobiography above, there is Issac Cline's account given in the Monthly Weather Review article by Garriott (1900). An additional account comes from a Mr. August Rollfing and is summarized in the book Issac's Storm, by Erik Larson (1999). After earlier sending his wife and children to his mother's house for safety, Mr. Rollfing found himself seeking refuge in the center of the city from rising water and wind-borne debris. He and two companions find refuge in a store, "that was crowded with about eighty men, women and children, all standing on countertops to keep out of the water. But the water was rising fast. August found a place on a counter. Soon the water was at his ankles, then his chest. August lifted someone else's son onto his shoulders as the water rose to his own neck.

He spent hours this way, until a man shouted, "The water is going down! Look at the door!"

The water had indeed reversed flow. The store owner pulled out a large jug of whiskey and passed it around the room. Men and women alike took great swallows and passed it on.

August wanted desperately to leave for his mother's house to join his wife and children and make sure they were still safe. The water receded quickly, but to him its exit seemed to take forever. Rain continued cascading from the darkness; the wind seemed little changed.

At last the water level fell low enough to enable him to leave. Outside, he saw that houses had been shattered and upended. He stumbled through deep holes gouged by the current and over all manner of submerged debris. He dodged showers of timber and slate. It was dark, no lights anywhere. He fell, got up, fell again. The damage got progressively worse. Whole blocks had been crushed, others swept clean. He knew he was heading west- probably along Avenue H- but the darkness and devastation had eliminated landmarks.

At intervals the moon emerged. How the moon could shine amid such wind and rain he did not know, but there it was, visible through a thin layer of cloud. A full moon, no less. It gave him light; it also gave him fear, for it showed him how vast the plane of devastation truly was. Spiky dunes of wreckage blocked his path. From the top of each, he saw that only a few homes still stood. To the south was a strange black shadow two and three stories high that stretched for miles like a mountain range freshly jabbed through the earth's crust.

At three o'clock Sunday morning he came to his mother's neighborhood. Only her house looked whole. Everything else had been destroyed, upended, or transported toward the bay. Relief poured into his heart. He burst into the house but found only his mother." (Editor's note: He later found his wife and children safe at his sister's house.)

DISCUSSION

The position of the center of the hurricane was estimated twice daily at 8 am and 8 pm Local Standard Time from an analysis of the surface pressure data from land stations along the U. S. Gulf of Mexico coastline. In the analysis, the hurricane was assumed to be represented by circular isobars out to approximately 1010 millibars and that the outer isobars represented by 1000 and 1005 millibars were approximately invariant in size as the hurricane moved across the Gulf of Mexico. Surprisingly, this gave a very reasonable track. The positions are shown in Figure 12.1 and are labeled with the date and time. It was estimated that these positions could vary by as much as one-half of a degree in any direction. The translational speed in miles per hour for a twelve hour time period between points was also plotted. As the hurricane moved away from Florida, it was being pushed westward by a high pressure ridge to the north and was moving at about 16 miles per hour. As it approached the western end of the ridge several days later, it began to slow and was moving about 9 miles per hour at landfall in Texas.

The actual landfall location has been debated ever since the hurricane occurred and will continue to be debated even after this report. The final landfall location was determined by both the meteorological and storm surge information from the observations above. The center must track near Quintana in order to produce the storm surge reported by Dr. Carlton. During the calm of the eye passage he waded in water up to his chin. The land elevations around Quintana were 3 to 4 feet above sea level and the height of his chin was assumed to be approximately 5 feet. This would make the water elevation 8 to 9 feet. The pressure reported by Captain Falfor at Quintana was 934.6 millibars and it was assumed that he was very close to the center. Therefore, the landfall pressure was set at 934 millibars. It seemed that the hurricane began a jog to the north just as it made landfall. The hurricane came ashore at 8:10 pm as reported by Dr. Carlton. Beginning at 8:00 pm the pressure bottoms out at Galveston, but remains there instead of rising immediately, as it would have if the hurricane had continued westward. The hurricane would also have begun to fill at this point and the only way to keep the pressure constant at Galveston until 8:30 pm is for the hurricane to have been moving toward the city. After 8:30 pm the filling would have been much faster. Even though the hurricane moved toward Galveston the pressure trace would have shown a rise. The hurricane was located very near the Brunner farm, located 8 miles west of Alvin, at about 12:30 am on the 9th of September. Thus, the track was turned northward after landfall and passed very close to the farm before turning back toward the northwest. After passing by the Brunner farm, the track was moved very close to the towns of Hempstead, Chapel Hill and Brenham which were "wrecked" by the hurricane. The estimated central pressure as it passed by was 989 to 994 millibars and the winds were probably gusting from 80 to 90 miles per hour.

Figure 12.2 is the track of the hurricane during landfall in Texas, with hourly positions and central pressure values plotted. The filling after landfall was determined by using a composite of filling rates from other historical hurricanes in Texas. The maximum measured wind at Quintana of 120 miles per hour and the estimated maximum wind at Galveston of 120 miles per hour are also noted. The value of the RMW could not be determined by the limited observations. The eyewitness accounts in Galveston do not suggest an eye wall passage. Most accounts from there have the wind blowing continuously and turning clockwise from the northeast to east to southeast and to south. The final value of the RMW was determined by successive iterations of the SLOSH model until the observed water elevations at both Galveston and Quintana agreed with the SLOSH model values. The final RMW is 27 statute miles. The RMW and circles representing the location of the maximum winds are shown in Figure 12.2. One was placed at the time of landfall and the other near the time of passage at the Brunner Farm. The maximum one-minute over the water wind from the SLOSH model at landfall was 132 miles per hour and is represented by the wind vector at the RMW.

SLOSH MODEL SIMULATION

The 1900 hurricane represented a major challenge because the water depths, land elevations and barriers in the SLOSH model are based upon current values. This includes the Galveston sea wall which was not present in 1900. Some excellent research work by Mr. Gene Hafele, Warning Coordination Meteorologist, at the Houston/Galveston National Weather Service Office resulted in 1900 elevations for Galveston Island and nearby areas. Dr. Wilson Shaffer at the Meteorological Development Laboratory at National Weather Service Headquarters in Silver Springs, Maryland took this information and created a 1900 SLOSH model grid. The zero datum for this new grid was mean sea level at that time, not NGVD. Therefore, the initial elevation was set at the height of the tide during landfall. From the historical tide model the hurricane made landfall near low tide and the initial water elevation was set at -0.5 feet.

A SLOSH model simulation was made with the track, intensity and RMW information shown in figure 12.2. As mentioned above this run was designed so that the SLOSH values agree with the observed values at the Church in downtown Galveston (11.7 feet) and

Quintana (8 to 9 feet). The SLOSH model values at these two locations are 11.8 feet and 8.4 feet respectively. The next step was to create a hydrograph from Issac Cline's account. Figure 12.3 is a plot of Cline's observations at his home where we know the elevations of the ground and first floor of his house (noted in Fig. 12.3). Also plotted is the SLOSH model hydrograph for the same location. Cline reported a steady rise of water until 7:30 pm when the height stood 8 inches above the floor of his home or approximately 12 feet. Then came a 4 foot up rush of water in 4 seconds. This was also reported by other nearby survivors. Everyone fled to the second story and the water rose another 5 feet in the next hour to 20 feet above mean sea level. There is no doubt that these values are correct. What is incorrect is the conclusion that all of this elevated water was due to storm surge. The SLOSH model hydrograph also shows a steady rise to 12 feet where it levels off and then begins to decrease after 9 pm. This SLOSH hydrograph would also apply to the location where August Rolfing was located, which was near the center of town and well back from the debris wall. The estimated height of the water where he was can be calculated thusly- the water was up to his neck or five feet above the counter top in the store. The counter top was approximately 3 feet above the floor and the floor was approximately 4 feet above mean sea level. This gives 12 feet above mean sea level. So the storm surge is approximately the same at both locations but Cline's location is affected by the moving wall of debris and the hurricane generated waves that are breaking over it.

The SLOSH model tells us a little about the wind generated waves and their angle of motion. The SLOSH model one-minute over the water wind speed and direction at the shoreline near Cline's house are; 3:30 pm-93/NE, 4:30 pm-97/ENE, 5:30 pm-102/E, 6:30 pm-107/ESE, 7:30 pm-110/SE, 8:30 pm-112/SE, 9:30 pm-111/SE, 10:30 pm-106/SE. The wind turns from the NE and comes around to the SE at 7:30 just as the first up rush of water occurs. The wind remained out of this direction until 11:30 pm when it turned to SSE. The storm surge reached its maximum from 8:00 to 9:00 pm when the highest additional elevations due to the breaking wave effects occurred. In this case it was approximately 8 feet at Cline's house. The house toppled over at about 8:30 pm and the struggle for survival began. Cline mentions that the water had gone down 4 feet by 11:30 pm. The SLOSH model hydrograph also showed a similar decrease by this time. Finally, August Rollfing is able to move about after 1 or 2 am, because he finally managed to struggle to his mother's house about 3 am, which means the water level had gone down below the land elevation. When the sun came up around 7 am, all the water was gone from the island.

The SLOSH model also revealed that the highest storm surges occurred inland and at the head of Galveston Bay. Many people probably lost their lives in small coastal settlements and farms. Very little information is available at these locations and in many instances it is very likely that everyone may have perished. The SLOSH model indicates that the surge penetrated 6 to 10 miles inland with many locations showing values of more than 18 feet above mean sea level. It is important to note that the depth of water at these locations is a function of the land above mean sea level. For instance, if a location inland is at a 12 foot elevation and had 18 feet of storm surge the height of the water above the ground would be 6 feet. The storm surge value at the head of Galveston Bay near the entrance to Buffalo Bayou, (which is the location of the Houston Ship Channel today), was almost 20 feet.

Late in the afternoon on Sunday, September 9, a train tried to reach Galveston. Eventually, it had to stop because water and debris covered the tracks and the engineer could not proceed safely. The train returned to Houston. Again, from <u>Isaac's Storm</u> a telegram was sent later that evening from Mr. G. L. Vaughan, who was the manager of the Western Union Office in Houston, to Mr. Willis Moore, Chief of the U.S. Weather Bureau. It stated, "First news from Galveston just received by train which could get no closer to the bay shore than six miles, where Prairie was strewn with debris and dead bodies. About two hundred corpses counted from train. Large steamship stranded two miles inland. Nothing could be seen of Galveston. Loss of life and property undoubtedly most appalling. Weather clear and bright here with gentle southeast wind."

SUMMARY FOR THE 1900 GALVESTON HURRICANE

The Galveston hurricane made landfall near Quintana, Texas or just south of Freeport, Texas on September 8, 1900 at approximately 8:10 pm Central Standard Time. The central pressure was measured at approximately 934 millibars at landfall. The radius of maximum winds was determined to be 27 statute miles. The maximum observed winds at Galveston were estimated to be 120 miles per hour and the maximum <u>measured</u> winds at Quintana were 120 miles per hour. The SLOSH generated one-minute over water winds at these two locations were 112 and 127 miles per hour respectively. The SLOSH model maximum wind at the RMW at landfall was 132 miles per hour.

The hurricane generated about a 12 foot storm surge over Galveston Island. Locations near a moving wall of debris experienced higher water elevations due to the effects of breaking waves over the debris pile. Locations closer to Galveston Bay and well behind this wall of debris experienced about 12 feet of storm surge.

As mentioned earlier, if this hurricane had been stronger or had been moving slower, then the entire island would have been swept clean and close to 20,000 people would have perished instead of 6,000.

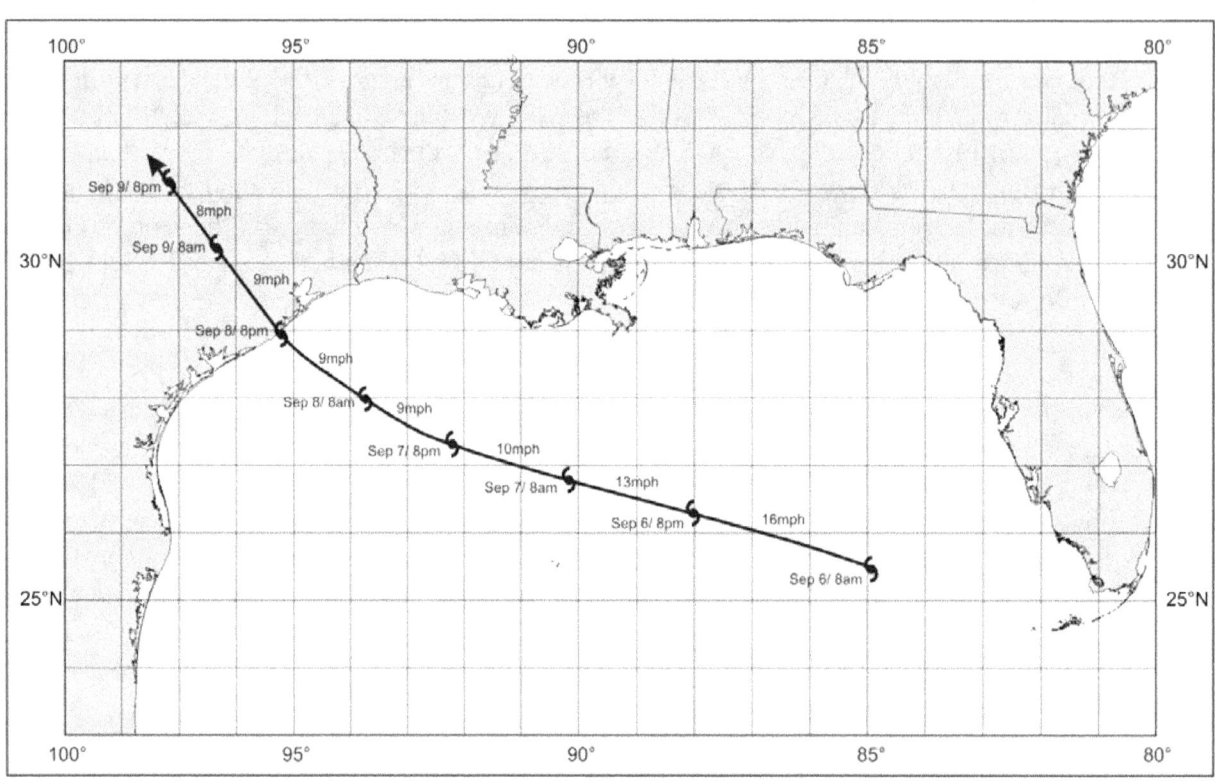

Figure 12.1 Track of the 1900 hurricane. 12-hourly positions at 8am and 8pm are plotted with date. Positions based upon surface pressure analysis. 12-hour translational speed given in miles per hour.

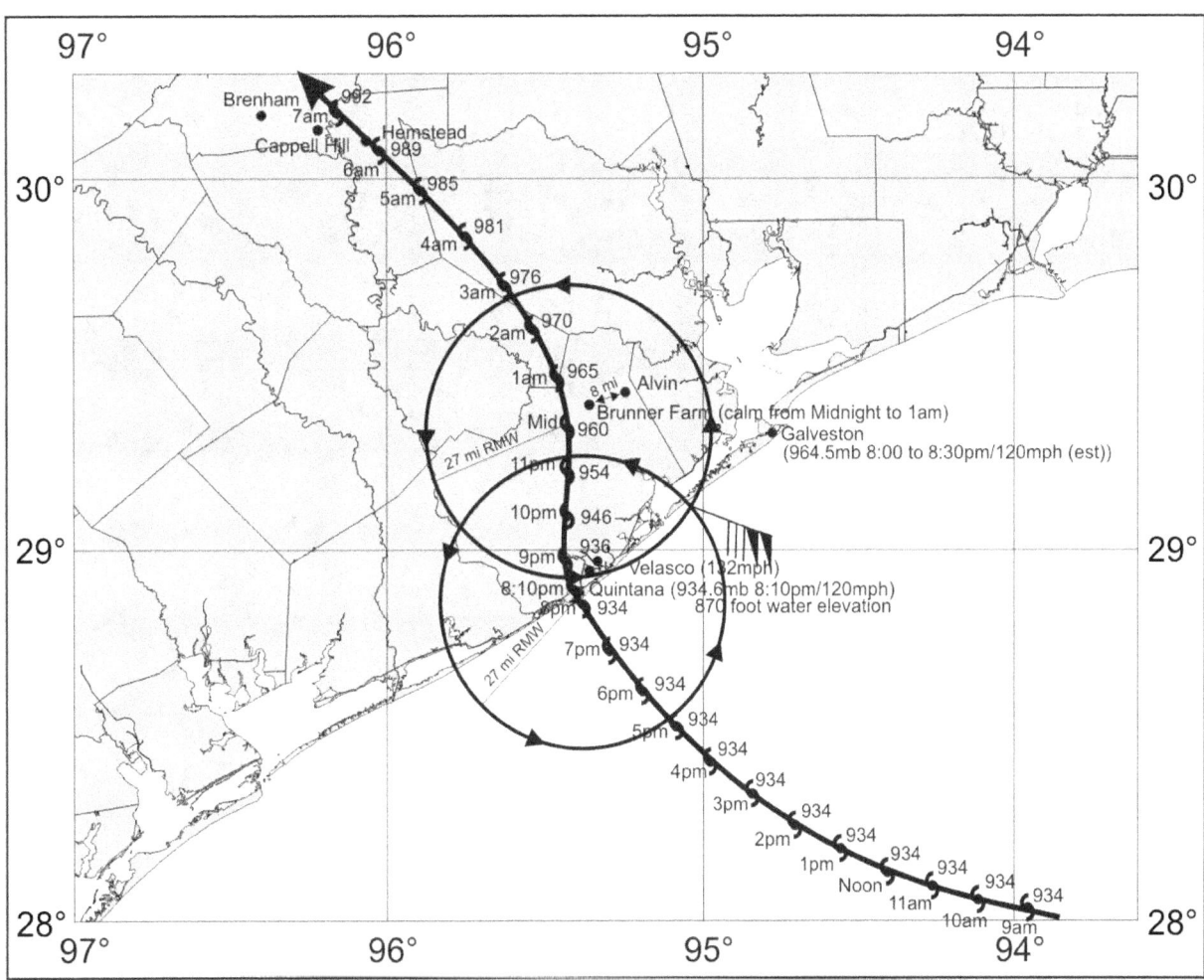

Figure 12.2 Track of the 1900 Galveston hurricane for September 8-9, 1900. Hourly positions are labeled in Local Standard Time and pressure in millibars. Circle with radial distance of 27 statute miles is the location of the maximum winds. Wind vector in miles per hour.

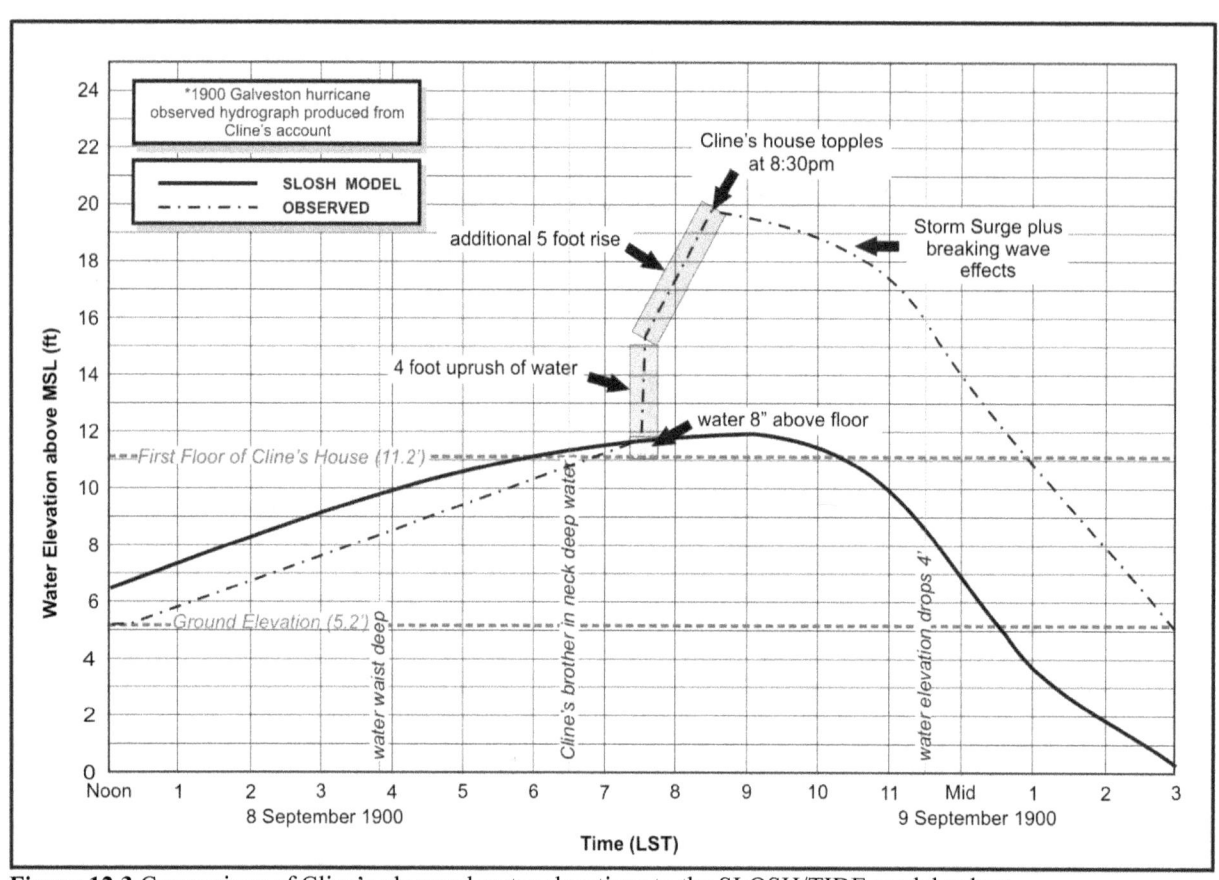

Figure 12.3 Comparison of Cline's observed water elevations to the SLOSH/TIDE model values.

SECTION 13

THE 1915 GALVESTON HURRICANE

The 1915 hurricane was a large category 4 hurricane as it approached the western side of the Gulf of Mexico. It appeared to be similar in size to hurricane Carla (1961) as it passed south of the Louisiana coast but, as Carla did, its RMW decreased as it approached the Texas coast. The hurricane made landfall near San Luis Pass at 1 am Local Standard Time on August 17 with an estimated central pressure of 930 millibars and a RMW of 11 statute miles. As was the case in the 1900 Galveston hurricane the storm tide was approximately 12 feet above mean sea level in Galveston and flooding took place in the city. However, the city was not destroyed like it was in 1900 because a sea wall had been built along the Gulf of Mexico shoreline to prevent the breaking waves from penetrating into the city. About 90% of the structures not protected by the sea wall were destroyed. Some structures near the southwest side of the city survived initially because they were protected by the sea wall when the wind was from the northeast and east. These structures were later destroyed when the wind shifted to the southwest and sent breaking waves in from that direction. Wave over wash on the seawall created scouring affects on the backside of the seawall and about 200 houses in the city collapsed. The sea wall was deemed a success and since 1915 it has been extended westward and both elevated and fortified.

METEOROLOGICAL DATA

The Monthly Weather Review article by Frankenfield (1915) was the main source of data for this hurricane. Pressure barographs were available for Galveston and Houston. Pressure observations were made and recorded at Velasco and a barograph was constructed from this data. The minimum pressure at Velasco was 952 millibars and occurred at 1 am on August 17. At Galveston the minimum occurred at 2:37 am and was 970 millibars and at Houston it occurred at 5:25 am and was 956 millibars.

The maximum winds at Galveston were 97 miles per hour from the east at 5:37 am. At Houston they occurred at 5:30 am and were estimated at 80 miles per hour from the northeast, and at 8:30 am they were estimated at 80 miles per hour from the southwest. (Note: There is an error in the wind directions in the article for the 8 am winds at both Houston and Galveston which should both be from the southwest). At Velasco the observer only had a wind vane and therefore only reported the direction of the wind, not the speed.

HYDROLOGIC DATA

A high water mark survey was conducted by the U.S. Army Corps in both Louisiana and Texas. In Louisiana the survey showed values ranging from 9 feet at Point au Fer located south of Morgan City in Atchafalaya Bay and up to 10.8 feet on the Louisiana side of Sabine Pass. In Texas the survey included locations in Galveston and Trinity Bays and on the outer coast to the south. Finally, 40 high water marks were taken in various structures in the City of Galveston.

DISCUSSION

Based upon the facts that the hurricane was able to produce significant storm tides along a large stretch of the Louisiana coastline, before it made landfall in Texas and with the track being fairly far to the south, meant that the system was not only intense by had a large RMW. This was similar to hurricane Carla (1961) which also generated high storm tide values in the same area. Carla tracked farther south then the 1915 hurricane and produced storm tide values along the Louisiana coast that ranged from 6 feet at Point Au Fer to 7.5 feet at Sabine Pass. Both hurricanes appeared to have central pressure values of 930 millibars and RMWs of approximately 30 to 40 statute miles as they tracked south of Louisiana. In both cases the RMW decreased as the hurricanes approached landfall in Texas, but in both cases it appears that the pressure remained approximately the same during this decrease in size. It appears to simply be an adjustment of the RMW with the attendant increase in wind speed due to a tighter pressure gradient.

The final landfall location was determined by several factors. First, the pressure at Velasco is 952 millibars and at Galveston 970 millibars. The center is closer to Velasco. Second, the wind directions with time reported by Velasco mean that the center can not be too close to Velasco or a northeast wind direction would have been reported as the hurricane approached landfall. Third, the author of the Monthly Weather Review article suggests that the hurricane made landfall near San Luis Pass. There might have been some information that was not noted in the Monthly Weather Review article that suggests a calm or lull in this vicinity. The track after landfall is well documented with calms and lulls as it progresses toward Houston. The center passes very close to Houston at 5:25 am and a 1 millibar correction is made to the pressure at Houston to give a central pressure at this time of 955 millibars. To determine the central pressure at 1 am when the hurricane was making landfall, the central pressure of 955 is adjusted backward at the standard filling rate that would have occurred during this time period. This gives a value of 930 millibars for the pressure at landfall. Figure 13.1 is the track of the 1915 hurricane with hourly values labeled in local standard time. The circles represent the location of the maximum winds. At 7 pm the RMW for the circle was 25 statute miles, at 10 pm it was 18 statute miles and at landfall the RMW was 11 statute miles. In all likelihood, this process probably continued and the RMW near Houston was probably around 6 to 7 miles which coincides with the damage pattern that occurred there.

To get a feel for the pressure gradient at landfall the radius of the isobars greater than 970 millibars were determined by noting what time the isobar of interest occurred in the Galveston barograph and then measuring the distance from Galveston to the track where this same time occurred. As mentioned earlier, the central pressure at landfall was determined to be 930 millibars. Figure 13.2 is an isobaric analysis of the hurricane at landfall. (Editor's Note: The 1000 millibar contour was not analyzed as it was at a greater distance than the figure.) The actual radial distance for the 1000 millibar contour was determined to be approximately 200 statute miles. The analysis inside of 950 millibars is purely subjective and it was assumed that the spacing between the 10 millibar pressure contours was decreasing to at least the RMW which was very close to the 940 millibar contour. The SLOSH model maximum one-minute over the water wind speed at the RMW at landfall is 151 miles per hour. It is shown as a wind vector in Figure 13.1 and 13.2. The SLOSH model wind comparison is shown for Galveston where the 93 mile per hour wind speed is compared to the 108 mile per hour SLOSH value.

SLOSH MODEL SIMULATION

The values in Figure 13.1 were used as input for the SLOSH model. In addition, the hurricane made landfall near high tide, but a small amplitude high tide, such that the initial datum was determined to be only about 0.6 feet in the Gulf of Mexico and 0.4 feet in Galveston Bay.

The value given by the SLOSH model in the city of Galveston was 12.4 feet. The 40 high water marks surveyed in Galveston ranged from 10.9 to 15.4 feet. The average of all forty marks was 12.4 feet. The fact that the values range about this mean value by plus or minus 20 percent is typical of observed high water mark data where localized influences can affect the final values. Table 13.1 shows a comparison of observed versus SLOSH model values at locations along the coast and inside Galveston Bay. All values are in feet above mean sea level.

TABLE 13.1

Location	Observed Height	SLOSH/Tide Height	(SLOSH- Observed)
Grand Cheniere, LA	10.0	9.2	-0.8
Cameron, LA	10.0	9.3	-0.7
Sabine Pass, LA	10.9	10.9	0.0
Port Bolivar, TX	11.5	11.6	0.1
Anahuac, TX	14.4	13.2	-1.2
Morgan's Point, TX	13.7	13.9	0.2
Seabrook, TX	15.4	14.4	-1.0
Texas City, TX	14.0	14.1	0.1
Freeport, TX	9.8	6.9	-2.9

In the 1900 hurricane the highest storm tide values occurred inside the bays and inland. The same is true for the 1915 hurricane as noted in Table 13.1. The highest storm tide value in the 1915 hurricane occurred inland behind Galveston Island and the SLOSH model calculated a value of almost 30.0 feet above sea level at this location. The land elevation where this value occurred was approximately 28.0 feet above sea level so that only 2 feet of salt water would appear above the ground for a short period of time before flowing back toward the Gulf of Mexico. Unfortunately, no survey was conducted in this area after the hurricane which could have verified this potential U. S record storm tide height.

SUMMARY FOR THE 1915 GALVESTON HURRICANE

The 1915 hurricane and 1900 hurricane had central pressures at landfall of 930 and 934 millibars respectively. However, the size of the RMW in each hurricane created very different wind fields at landfall. The 1915 and 1900 hurricanes had RMWs of 11 and 27 statute miles respectively. Because the 1900 hurricane made landfall about 21 statute miles southwest of where the 1915 did, the maximum winds in both hurricanes passed over the southwestern portion of Galveston Island. The SLOSH model maximum one-minute over the water wind speed at Galveston for the 1915 and 1900 hurricanes were 108 and 112 miles per hour respectively. This is part of the reason for the similar storm tide values at Galveston which were 12.4 feet for the 1915 hurricane and 11.8 feet for the 1900 hurricane.

Based upon the SLOSH model results for these two historical hurricanes in the Galveston area-federal, state and local emergency management should review their evacuation scenarios to assure that the potential storm tide flood zones inland have been adequately addressed.

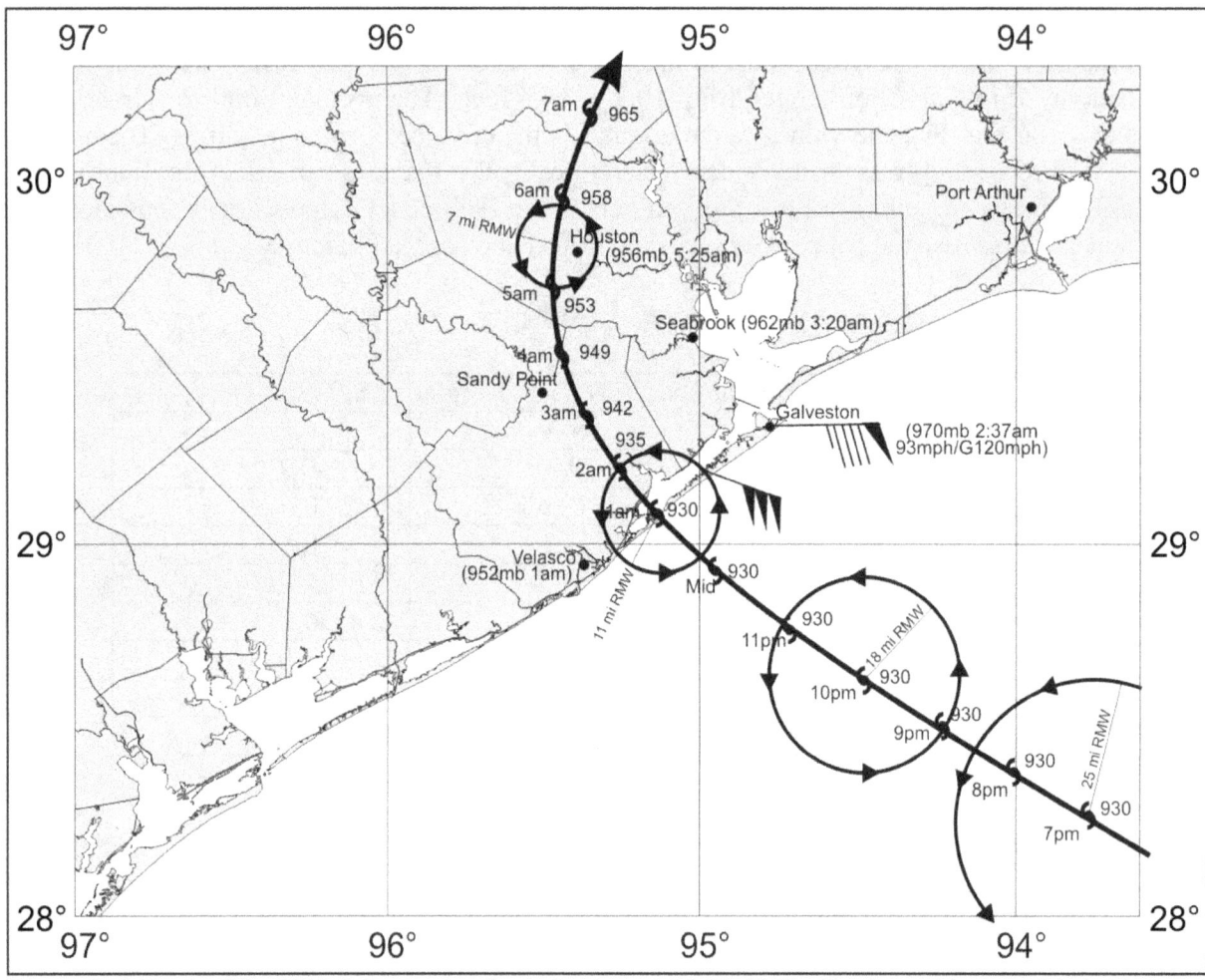

Figure 13.1 Track of the 1915 Galveston hurricane for August 16-17, 1915. Hourly positions are labeled in Local Standard Time and pressure in millibars. Circles, with radial distance in statute miles, are the location of the maximum winds. Wind vector in miles per hour. Observed wind and pressure data at labeled locations.

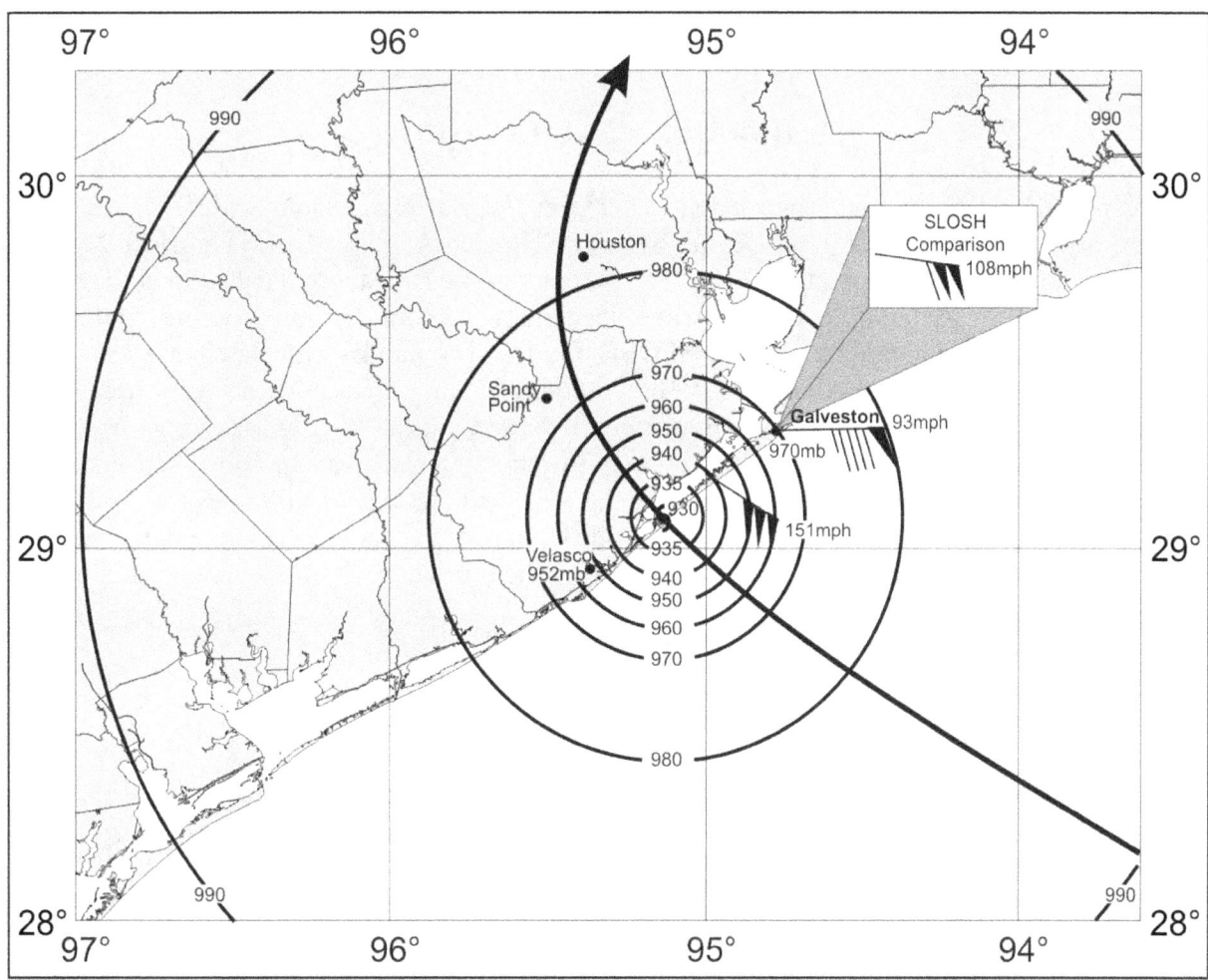

Figure 13.2 Surface pressure analysis for the 1915 Galveston hurricane. At Galveston the observed wind vector is compared to the SLOSH vector.

SECTION 14

HURRICANE ALICIA 1983

Hurricane Alicia was a borderline category 2/3 on the Saffir/Simpson Scale when it made landfall near San Luis Pass at 1 am Central Standard Time on August 18. This hurricane was the first hurricane where an operational SLOSH model run was made at the National Hurricane Center to provide guidance to the hurricane specialists. About 12 hours before landfall the forecaster provided input data for the SLOSH model. The model calculated a storm surge ranging from 10 to 12 feet in Galveston Bay and surrounding areas. These were used in the storm surge sections of the hurricane advisories. It turned out that the track forecast was good, but the forecast wind speed was about 10 knots too high. As a result the observed maximum storm surge was somewhat lower than the SLOSH predictions. Still, several low lying communities at the head of Galveston were flooded. In some of these locations people failed to heed evacuation orders and were later rescued during the hurricane by emergency personnel.

METEOROLOGICAL DATA

Note: All times will be referenced to Central Standard Time.

A preliminary report was available for this hurricane in the National Hurricane Center archives. The hurricane formed in the Gulf of Mexico on the tail end of a frontal trough on August 15, 1983. The system moved slowly toward the west for a day and a-half and began to intensify. It then began a slow turn toward the northwest, continued to intensify and made landfall on August 18 as a border line category 2/3. At landfall it was moving at about 8 miles per hour. It moved up the west side of Galveston Bay pushing water toward the head of the bay. It continued to move toward the northwest and dissipated several days later.

The minimum pressure at Galveston was 989 millibars at 2 am and at the National Weather Service Office in Alvin it was 967 millibars at 4:25 am. The maximum sustained wind and gust at Galveston were 71/98 miles per hour at 1:17 am and at Alvin it was 48/73 miles per hour at 1:35 am. Alvin also recorded a minimum wind speed of 14 miles per hour at 4:25 am when the eye of the hurricane passed over.

The Hurricane Research Division of the Atlantic Oceanographic and Meteorological Laboratories was conducting research missions by aircraft and at ground based radar sites. Many of their finding were included in the report titled, "Hurricane Alicia, Galveston and Houston, Texas, August 17-18, 1983", which was produced by the Committee on Natural Disasters of the National Research Council. The report also included information about wind damage to various structures including buildings along the coastline and high-rise buildings in Houston.

HYDROGRAPHIC DATA

The U.S. Army Corps of Engineers produced a report titled, "Hurricane Alicia, 15-18 August 1983". This report contained a summary of the high water marks recorded during a post hurricane survey. In addition, it contained hydrographs from tide gages at various locations in the region.

The highest observed storm tide occurred inland behind Galveston Island and was 12.1 feet above NGVD. In Galveston Bay the maximum water elevations occurred at the head of the Bay and were 10 to 11 feet above NGVD.

DISCUSSION

Figure 14.1 is a plot of the track of Hurricane Alicia with hourly positions plotted in Local Standard Time and central pressure values in millibars. The hurricane makes landfall at 1 am near San Luis Pass with a central pressure of 962 millibars. The reconnaissance aircraft was able to make another center fix at 2 am and reported that the eye was over land and that the pressure was still 962 millibars. At 4:25 am the center was just to the southwest of Alvin which reported a 967 millibar pressure and a wind speed of 14 miles per hour. At this time the central pressure was estimated to be 1 millibar less or 966 millibars. After 5 am the filling rate increased as the system continued to move inland.

The radar presentations in the report by the Committee on Natural Disasters suggest a double eye wall before landfall that disappeared during landfall and reappeared after landfall. During landfall the radar showed a single eye wall that was approximately 19 statute miles from the center. The circles in Figure 14.1 are the locations of the maximum winds at selected times. The RMW for both circles is19 statute miles and is the value used in the SLOSH model run.

SLOSH MODEL RUN

Using the observed tide hydrographs it was determined that the hurricane and its associated storm surge arrived near high tide. The added water in the Gulf of Mexico at high tide would be 1.1 feet. The correction for the rise of mean sea level from NGVD is 0.3 feet. This gives a total initial water elevation of 1.4 feet for the Gulf of Mexico. Inside the bay the initial value was slightly less because the tide range was less and a value of 1.0 foot was used. A SLOSH model simulation was made with the information given in Figure 14.1.

Four tide hydrographs from four gages were selected for comparison with the SLOSH model, using data from the Army Corps of Engineers report. The locations of the four gages are shown in Figure 14.2. The Pleasure Pier gage is representative of water elevation changes in the Gulf of Mexico in front of the Galveston sea wall. Pier 21 is representative of the Galveston ship channel. Seabrook is representative of the middle of the bay and Baytown Exxon is representative of the head of the bay and the entrance to the Houston ship channel. The comparisons are shown in Figures 12.3 to 12.6. Overall the comparisons are good except at Pier 21. Here the SLOSH model hydrograph is about 2 feet higher than observed. High water marks nearby also support the tide gage value. One possible explanation is that the wind speeds generated in the SLOSH model were higher than what actually occurred. To investigate this possibility the SLOSH model maximum wind speed at Galveston (107 miles per hour) was compared to the observed maximum (71 miles per hour). Certainly this helps to explain why there is a lower observed storm tide value at Pier 21 versus the SLOSH value. However, the same SLOSH wind speed produced the SLOSH result at the Pleasure Pier, which agreed well with the observed gage result. Additional work needs to be done to determine why the difference exists. This may require a SLOSH model adjustment in the Galveston ship channel.

SUMMARY FOR HURRICANE ALICIA

Hurricane Alicia was a borderline category 2/3 on the Saffir/Simpson scale when it made landfall in Texas. The SLOSH model maximum one-minute over the water wind at landfall at the RMW was 112 miles per hour versus 115 miles per hour for the observed maximum. At Galveston the maximum wind was 71 miles per hour versus the SLOSH wind of 107 miles per hour which is quite a difference. The highest observed storm tide occurred inland behind Galveston Island and was 12.1 feet. At this location the SLOSH model calculated 12.1 feet. In Galveston Bay, the highest storm tides of 10 to 11 feet occurred at the head of the bay near the entrance to the Houston ship channel.

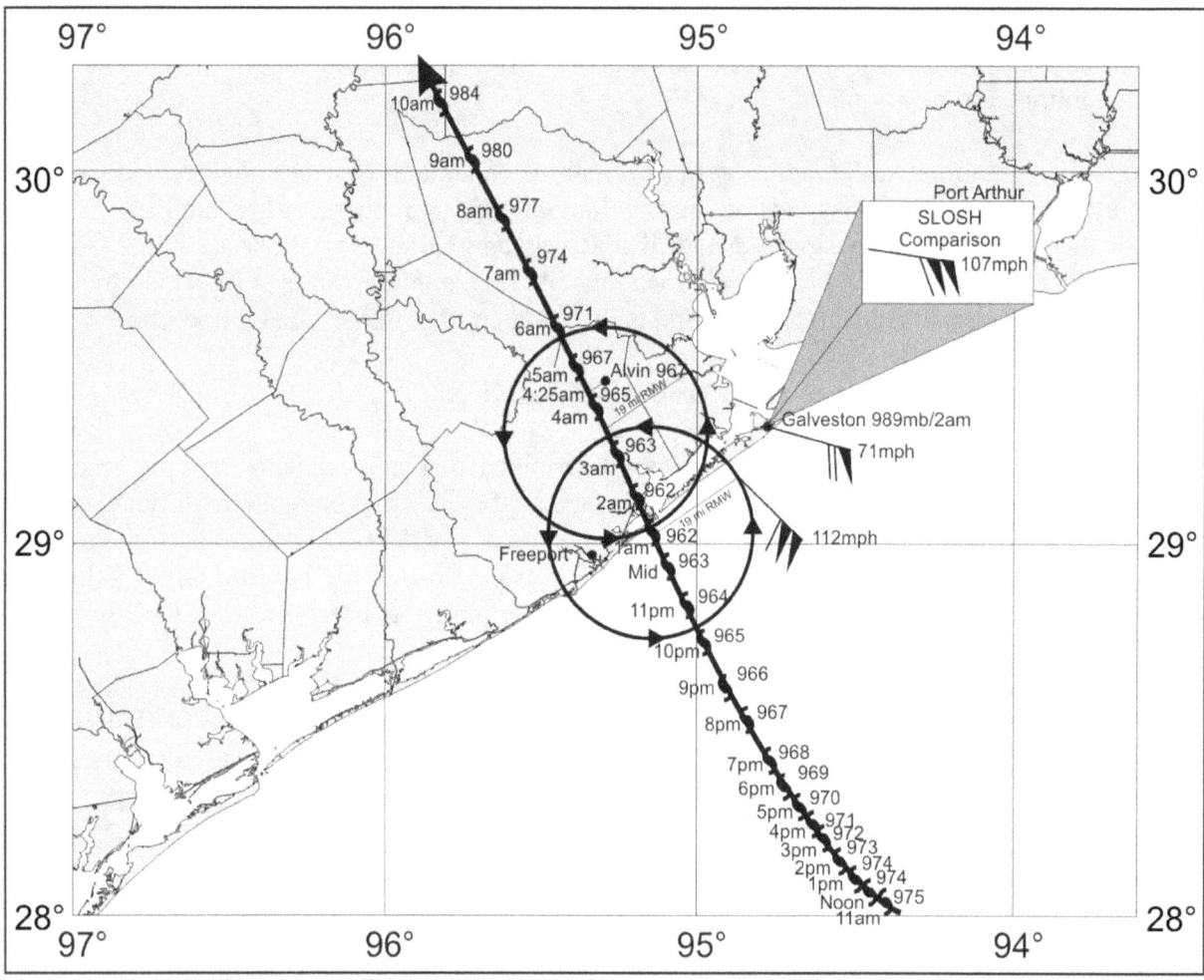

Figure 14.1 Track of hurricane Alicia, August 17-18, 1983. Hourly positions are labeled in Local Standard Time and pressure in millibars. Circles, with radial distance in statute miles, are the location of the maximum winds. Wind vector in miles per hour. Observed and SLOSH calculated wind are compared at Galveston.

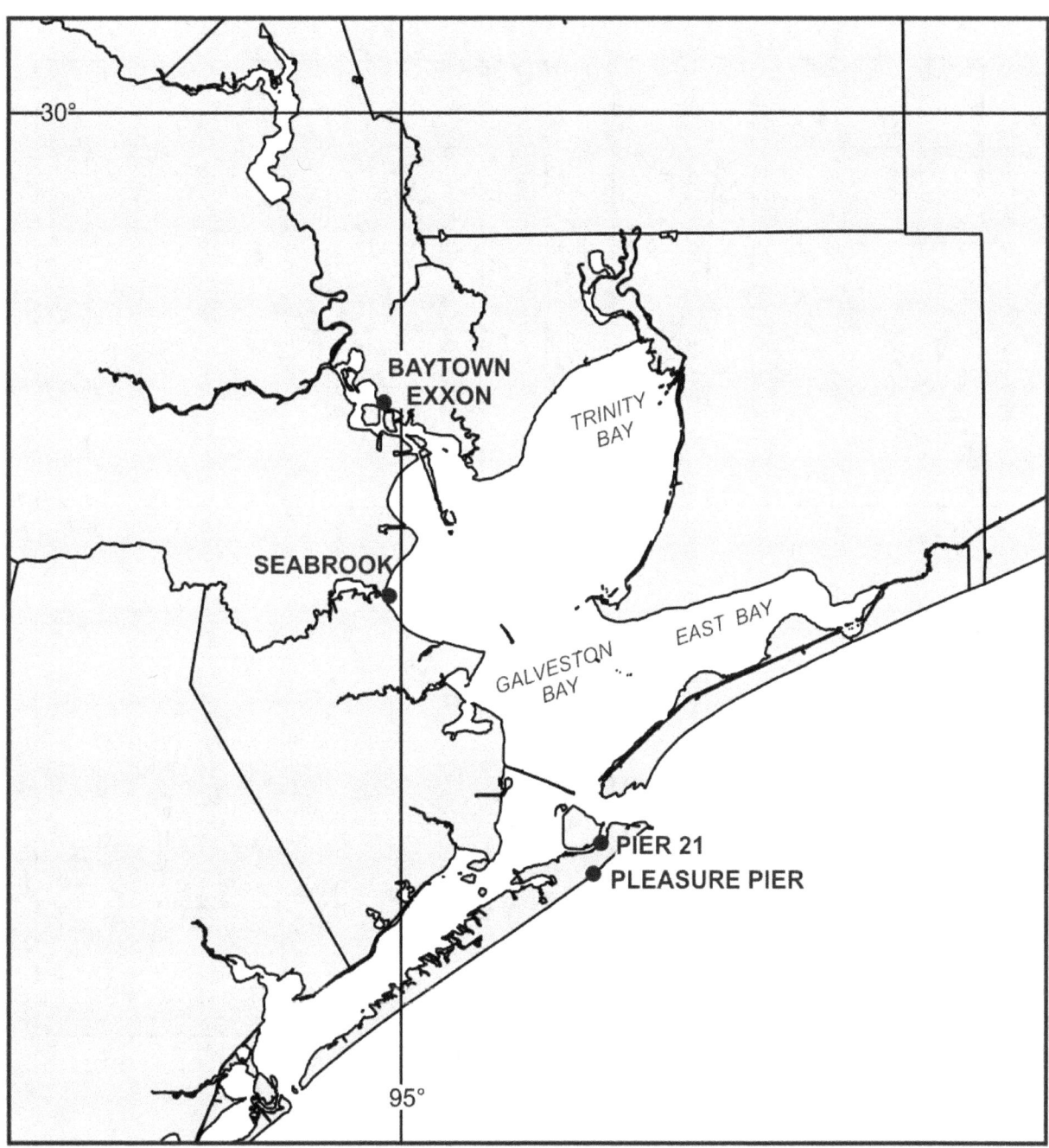

Figure 14.2 Location of tide gages during hurricane Alicia, 1983.

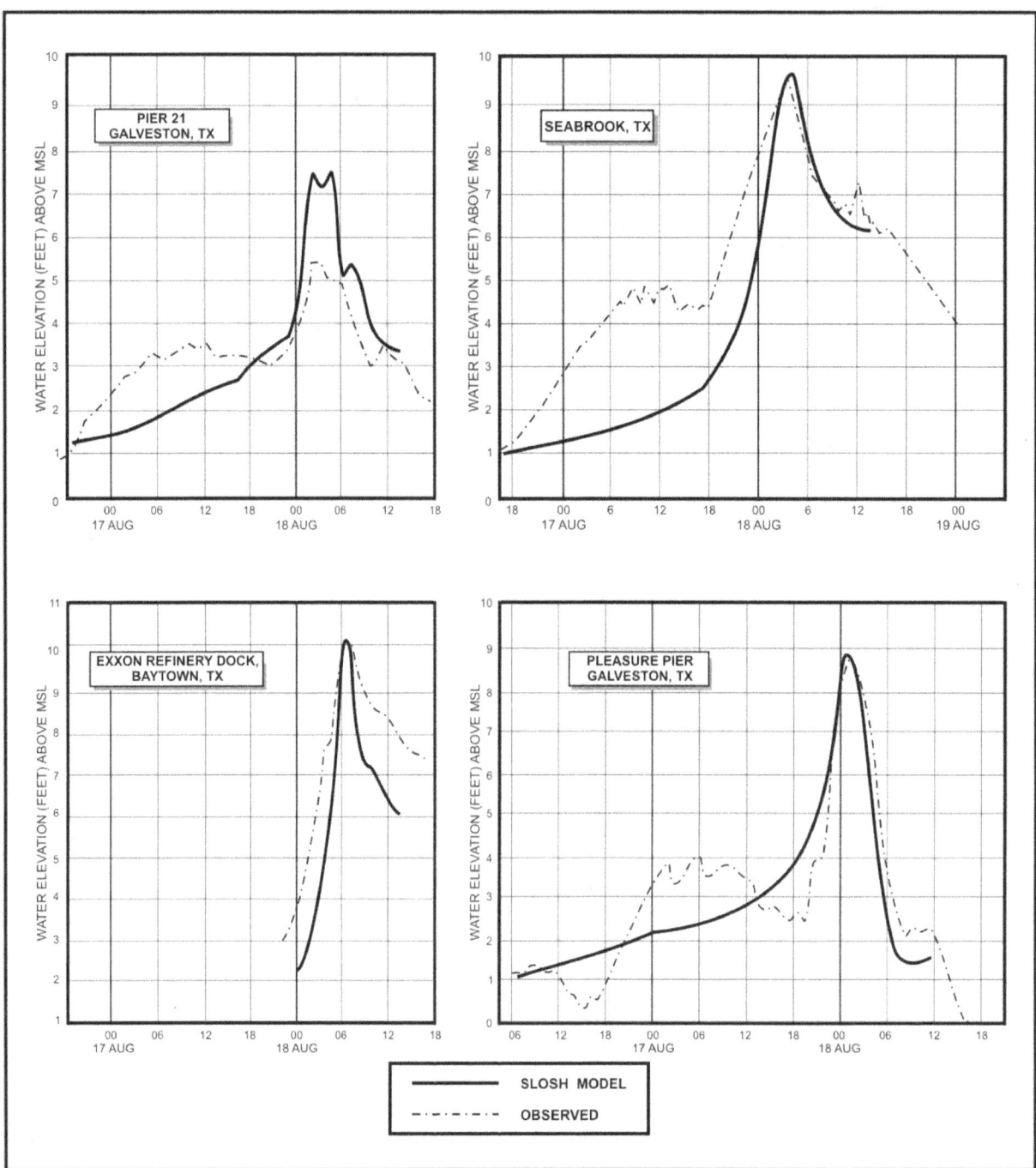

Figure 14.3 Comparison of observed and SLOSH/TIDE model hydrographs at four locations.

REFERENCES

Avila, L., 2002: "Tropical Cyclone Report, Hurricane Isidore, 14 – 27 September, 2002", National Hurricane Center, Miami, Florida. 14 pp.

Bradford, W., 1647: Of Plymouth Plantation 1620-1647, Morison, S.E., ed., 1952, pp 279-280.

Davis, W. R., 1954: "Hurricanes of 1954", Monthly Weather Review, Vol. 82, No. 12, pp. 370-373.

Frankenfield, H. C., 1915: "The West Indian Hurricane of 1915", Monthly Weather Review, Vol. 43, No. 8, pp 405-412.

Garriott, E. B., 1900: "West Indian Hurricane of September 1-12, 1900", Monthly Weather Review, Vol. 28, No. 9, pp 371-377.

Harris, D. L., 1958: Hurricane Audrey Storm Tide, National Hurricane Research Project, Report No. 23, Washington, D.C., 19 pp.

Harris, D. L., 1963: "Characteristics of the Hurricane Storm Surge", Weather Bureau Technical Paper No. 48, Washington, D.C., 139 pp.

Ho, F. P., 1989: "Extreme Hurricanes in the Nineteenth Century", NOAA Technical Memorandum NWS HYDRO 43A, 134 pp.

Jelesnianski, C. P., J. Chen and W. A. Shaffer, 1992: "SLOSH: Sea. Lake and Overland Surges from Hurricanes", NOAA Technical Report NWS48, Silver Springs, MD, 71 pp.

Larson, E., 1999: Issac's Storm, Crown Publishers, 201 East 50th St. New York, New York, 10022, 323 pp.

Lawrence, M. B., 2002: "Cyclone Report, Hurricane Lili, 21 September – 04 October, 2002", National Hurricane Center, Miami, Florida. 14 pp.

Ludlam, D. M., 1963: Early American Hurricanes 1492-1870, Published and sold by the American Meteorological Society, 45 Beacon Street, Boston 8, Massachusetts, 198 pp.

Marscher, Bill and Fran, 2001: The Great Sea Island Storm of 1893, Authors Choice Press, iUniverse.com, Inc., 5220 S 16th, Ste. 200, Lincoln, NE 68512.

McDonald, W. F., 1935: "The Hurricane of August 31 to September 6, 1935", Monthly Weather Review, Vol. 63, No. 9, pp 269-289.

McGuire, J. K., 1954: "Hurricane Carol, August 26-31, 1954", Climatological Data National Summary, Vol. 5, No. 8, pp. 289-292.

Moore, P. L. and Staff, 1957: "The Hurricane Season of 1957", Monthly Weather Review, Vol. 85, No. 12, pp 401-406.

Myers, V. A. and Jordan, E. S., 1956: "Winds and Pressure over the Sea in the Hurricane of September 1938", Monthly Weather Review, Vol. 84, No. 7, pp. 261-270.

Pierce, C. H., 1939: "The Meteorological History of the New England Hurricane of September 21, 1938", Monthly Weather Review, Vol. 67, No. 8, pp. 237-285.

Rhodes, C. E., 1954: "North Atlantic Hurricanes and Tropical Disturbances", Climatological Data National Summary, Vol. 5, No. 13, pp. 72-88.

Ross, R.B. and Blum, M. D., 1957: "Hurricane Audrey, 1957", Monthly Weather Review, Vol. 85, No. 6, pp 221-227.

Tannehill, I. R., 1938: "Hurricane of September 16 to 22, 1938", Monthly Weather Review, Vol. 66, No. 9, pp. 286-288.

U. S. Army Corps of Engineers, 1956: Appraisal Report, Hurricanes Affecting the Florida Coast, Hurricane of August 31-September 8, 1935, B12-17.

Wexler, R., 1939: "The Filling of the New England Hurricane of September 1938", Bulletin of the American Meteorological Society, Vol. 20, No. 7, pp. 277-281.

Winthrop, J., 1649: The History of New England from 1630-1649, Savage J., ed., 1853, pp 195-198.

ACKNOWLEDGEMENTS

The project would not have been possible without the executive decisions of director, Max Mayfield, and deputy director, Ed Rappaport. Thank you, gentlemen.

The Staff at the National Hurricane Center was very supportive of this project. In particular, Dr. Stephen Baig provided excellent guidance as well as staff support to make the myriad of SLOSH model runs required to understand the hurricane storm surge. I certainly taxed the patience of the young ladies in the storm surge group. Thank you Gloria Lockett, Jennifer Pralgo and Tarah Sharon.

Dr. Wilson Shaffer and his staff, at the Meteorological Development Laboratory in Silver Springs, MD, provided the SLOSH basin adjustments for several of the historical hurricanes. This is very tedious work and I thank you all for your help.

On some of the very early hurricanes that were investigated, I needed reality checks on the meteorology and these were provided by Jack Bevin and Richard Pasch. You gentlemen know your science and history. Your expertise is much appreciated.

The NOAA library system contains a wealth of historical information but without the help of Gloria Aversano, Librarian, it would have been almost impossible to navigate the system. Finding the 1776 survey of the potential site of the Cape Cod Canal, commissioned by George Washington, was an astounding piece of detective work. Thanks, Gloria.

The drafted figures are readable because I didn't do them. Their professional quality was produced by Joan David. Thank you, Joni.

Proofreading and editing was provided by my wife, Diane and my father-in-law, Bill Hackett. Thank you both for your tireless efforts to make this a readable report.

The final list of individuals each played a part in certain particular hurricanes. Mr. Rodger Menzeis, U.S. Army Corps of Engineers Savannah District, Mr. William Winn, Emergency Management Director, Beaufort County, SC, Mr. Al Sandrik, Jacksonville Weather Forecast Office, Mr. Greg Hammer, National Climatic Data Center, Ashville, NC, Mr. Frank Revitte, New Orleans Weather Forecast Office, Mr. Bill Read and Mr. Gene Hafele of the Houston/Galveston Weather Forecast Office, Mr. Billy Wagner, Monroe County Emergency Management and Mr. Lew Fincher, of Hurricane Consulting, Inc. Thank you all for your help.

Finally, thanks to all those who helped with this project that I somehow neglected to mention.

www.ingramcontent.com/pod-product-compliance
Lightning Source LLC
Chambersburg PA
CBHW052004280526
45793CB00005B/844